how to be better at...

managing change

D E Hussey

<u>YOURS TO HAVE AND TO HOLD</u>
BUT NOT TO COPY

First published in 1998

Kogan Page Limited
120 Pentonville Road
London N1 9JN

© David Hussey, 1998

British Library Cataloguing in Publication Data
A CIP record of this book is available from the British Library.
ISBN 07494 2562 8

Typeset by Kogan Page Ltd
Printed and bound in Great Britain by Clays Ltd, St Ives plc

THE INDUSTRIAL SOCIETY

The Industrial Society stands for changing people's lives. In nearly eighty years of business, the Society has a unique record of transforming organizations by unlocking the potential of their people, bringing unswerving commitment to best practice and tempered by a mission to listen and learn from experience.

The Industrial Society's clear vision of ethics, excellence and learning at work has never been more important. Over 10,000 organizations, including most of the companies that are household names, benefit from corporate Society membership.

The Society works with these, and non-member organizations, in a variety of ways – consultancy, management and skills training, in-house and public courses, information services and multimedia publishing. All this with the single vision to unlock the potential of people and organizations by promoting ethical standards, excellence and learning at work.

If you would like to know more about the Industrial Society please contact us.

The Industrial Society
48 Bryanston Square
London W1H 7LN
Telephone 0171 262 2401

The Industrial Society is Registered Charity No. 290003

HOW TO BE A BETTER... SERIES

In recognition of this and sharing their commitment to management development at all levels, Kogan Page and The Industrial Society have joined forces to publish the How to be a Better... series.

Designed specifically with your needs in mind, the series covers all the core skills you need to make your mark as a high-performing and effective manager.

Enhanced by mini case studies and step-by-step guidance, the books in the series are written by acknowledged experts who impart their advice in a practical way which encourages effective action.

Now you can bring your management skills up to scratch and give your career prospects a boost with the How to be a Better... series!

Titles available are:
How to be Better Communicator
How to be a Better Decision Maker
How to be a Better at Giving Presentations
How to Hold Better Meetings
How to be a Better Interviewer
How to be Better at Motivating People
How to be a Better Negotiator
How to be a Better Problem Solver
How to be a Better Project Manager
How to be a Better Teambuilder
How to be a Better Time Manager
How to be Better at Writing Reports and Proposals

Available from all good booksellers. For further information on the series, please contact:

Kogan Page, 120 Pentonville Road, London N1 9JN
Tel: 0171 278 0433   Fax: 0171 837 6348

CONTENTS

1

INTRODUCTION

Management is, to a large degree, about making things happen. Decisions are of little value unless they lead to actions, and strategies do nothing for an organization until they are implemented. Although many decisions and some strategies do not require the organization to change, there are many that depend heavily on change management skills.

Although the major changes – such as those that have taken place in the utilities after privatization – should be led from the top, many aspects of the changes may be managed by other managers at various levels throughout the organization. But change management is not restricted to the huge changes that hit the news headlines.

Organizations are constantly undergoing numerous smaller changes, which may be initiated at points throughout the organizational hierarchy.

Any decision that requires people to do different things or to do things differently, to apply different skills, or which enlarges or reduces the headcount may call for a measure of change management competence. Anything that involves many people or crosses departmental borders may require an even higher level of such competence.

FORCES FOR CHANGE

The environment in which organizations operate has become ever more turbulent, forcing organizations to adapt and modify themselves in order to continue to survive and prosper. Because the frequency of environmental change has steadily increased over the past few decades, and its impact on organizations becomes ever more severe, change management skills have become an important weapon in a manager's armoury. It is not that organizational change itself is more important now than it used to be, but that it happens more often, and the period of stability after the change does not last as long as it once did. All the signs are that the pace of change will continue to accelerate as we move into the next century. There can be few managers who have not had some involvement in a change situation in their organizations, and the expectation is that the number of change situations faced in a career will increase.

Among the external forces that help to cause this situation are:

❏ *Competition* There is more of it about, and an organization's size is little protection. In many industries, competitors think of markets in world terms, and there is always someone out to displace your established position. This requires organizations to be competitive globally, to pay more attention to customer requirements, and to innovate more frequently. More attention has to be paid to competitors, and the ways in which competitive advantage can be gained and sustained.

❏ *Customers* Expectations have changed and customers are more demanding and less willing to tolerate poor service or products that do not match the promised quality. Many industrial customers have moved to a more cooperative role with their preferred suppliers, and both organizations have to change continuously in order to enable the demands of the final consumers to be met.

❏ *Technology* Development costs for new products tend to increase, but their lifecycle shortens. This means that organizations have to be willing to kill products and replace them with more advanced products before they reach the point where market share is lost to a competitor. New processes must regularly be applied, to prevent the organization from being outclassed by competitors. Technologies merge. Once, for example, there was a computer industry and a typewriter industry and their products did not compete with each other. Today, most business typing is done on computers, which have also merged with telecommunications. These develop-ments alter how people manage in organizations, and how they perform their daily tasks. Much of what is routine today was unthought of only two decades ago. Costs of developing new high-tech products continue to rise, forcing organiza-tions into alliances with firms that may once have been com-petitors and to change both what they do and how they do it.

❏ *Deregulation* In most countries, there has been a removal of regulations that protected the inefficient and a move to pri-vatize businesses that were in the public sector and create a competitive environment within those public-sector activi-ties that cannot be privatized. This has brought massive change to organizations such as telephone companies, hos-pitals, water utilities in many EU countries, and to the whole industrial structure in Central European countries such as Hungary. In turn this has an effect on the businesses that deal with these organizations.

Enough has been said to suggest that the forces of change are moving faster and have greater impact than they did for yester-day's managers – and that tomorrow's managers will be able to make the same statement.

THE IMPORTANCE OF EFFECTIVE CHANGE MANAGEMENT

Most changes that organizations have to undergo are vital for future success. Indeed, some may be critical if the organization is to survive. All should be important for if they are not, there is lit-tle point in making the change.

If the change is managed badly, the outcome is likely to dis-appoint. At worst, when the change is urgent and critical, the organization may fail, leading to bankruptcy or acquisition by another firm. It may be that the change does not achieve as good a result as was hoped, because a window of opportunity is missed, costs rise higher than first thought or employee morale slumps, leading to a fall in productivity. The organization may survive this, but be in a weaker position than if the change had gone smoothly. Not all changes are critical, but all can fail if they are badly managed, with similar problems of missed deadlines, higher costs, reduced results and wasted effort.

Change can be associated with loss of jobs, changes in future prospects for employees and a negation of much past work involved in building up people's experience and skills. The potential for disruption of the lives of employees may be high in a well-handled change; in a badly managed change, this disruption may be magnified. Any manager worthy of the title has a duty to ensure that changes are implemented with the least possible harm to employees. This does not mean shirking the task of dealing with necessary things that adversely affect people, but it does mean not making things worse by ineffective management. And some managers do make things worse.

Some support for these remarks comes from findings from research. Since the 1960s, research has been undertaken regularly by different people into the success rate for acquisitions, a change activity that impacts on both the acquired company and the acquirer. The findings are remarkably consistent: only 50 per cent succeed, which means that 50 per cent fail. Sometimes this failure means the closing down of the acquired company, and sometimes its disposal, possibly at a capital loss, after a period of annual losses. Just think of all the estate agents acquired by building societies and insurance companies in the UK in the late 1980s, many of which were sold off at huge losses during the 1990s. Whatever was expected from the original change initiatives did not happen. In the USA, the great retailer Sears Roebuck had equally disastrous results from its acquisition of estate agents and merchant banking companies in what was hoped would be a revolution in financial services: at the same time the company also bought a Dutch freight forwarder, a British based timber importer, and various other activities in a failed attempt to create a global trading enterprise.

Other research in the 1990s shows that only a fraction of Total Quality Management (TQM) initiatives have met their objectives; only about a quarter to a third of corporate downsizing activity has brought better profits than comparable competitors that have not downsized; and the success rate from Business Process Re-engineering (BPR) lies between 30 and 50 per cent.

These are the high-profile changes, but most readers will be able to add numerous smaller examples from their own experience: the new product that was late reaching the market; the new computer process that brought chaos and confusion instead of benefit; the sales force restructure that seemed to add little to results.

To start you thinking about change, before you read further, you might like to contemplate a change you have experienced or managed in your own present or past organization. If you are one of the rare people who has seen no changes, you may like to think of one of the companies that has been described in press articles or one where a friend works. Jot down your answers to the following questions, and keep the answers in mind as we move further into the change management issue.

Your experience of change

1. Describe the change.

What was it?

How urgent was it?

How important was it?

2. Did it succeed:

completely?   ☐

partly?   ☐

or did it fail?   ☐

3. What were the main reasons for the results that were achieved?

4. List up to six things that were done well.

5. List up to six things that could have been done better.

HOW THE BOOK IS ORGANIZED

Chapter 2 offers some principles for change management. The first of these is that the way a change is managed should be fitted to the situation. Factors that affect what the appropriate approach in a given situation will be are examined. This chapter will also introduce you to the EASIER approach to change management (this is an acronym that makes it easier to remember the headings that can help you in this task). A key factor of the approach is that it gives attention to the behavioural and system/analytical aspects of change management.

In Chapter 3, more attention is given to assessing the implications of a change situation, with checklists to help you identify and diagnose particular situations. We will also look at the impediments to change and how they might be dealt with.

One potential impediment that requires specific attention is resistance to change. Chapter 4 examines two problem areas. First, there is the prevalent issue of the causes of resistance and what might be done to overcome them. A second, and sometimes related issue, is managing the survivors of change. When a change results in redundancies, attention needs to be given to the motivation of survivors, who may experience anger, resentment and even guilt – all of which can damage morale and affect performance and the continued success of the change.

Chapter 5 explores what is involved in applying the EASIER model – an exploration continued in the final chapter, which shows how the model could be applied in a case study situation.

The final chapter continues with a discussion of some of the personal skills needed to be an effective change leader, and what a manager can do if some of the skills are lacking.

Throughout, the aim is to provide practical examples, short case studies and checklists to make the concepts clear, and to aid their transfer to your own particular situation.

2

CHOOSING THE RIGHT LEVEL OF PARTICIPATION

There is a commonly held view that if the people affected are involved in a change, it will go smoothly. Sometimes involvement is spoken of as if it were all that needed to be done. It is a fallacy to assume that involvement is appropriate for, or even possible in, all change situations. In any case, we are left with choices to make about what we mean by involvement. Do we mean helping to make the decision about the change, helping to determine how to implement a predetermined decision, being consulted but not playing a real part in the process or just being informed? Also who should be involved, and should the type of involvement be the same from top to bottom of the organization?

In this chapter, we will explore a contingency approach, that is, we shall examine how the situation might alter the style used to manage change. This will be followed by an introduction to an approach to successful change management, which has value in all change situations, although the choice of style will affect how it is applied.

MODIFYING THE APPROACH TO FIT THE SITUATION

'Style' has been used for want of a better word, but what is really meant is the choice of one of many possible positions on a spectrum varying from totally democratic to totally autocratic. We should be willing to consider modifying the style as we work with different groups of people. In this chapter, the spectrum of involvement is simplified to four styles. There is no one style that is always right, and change management is likely to be more effective if a style is selected to fit the requirements of the situation.

It is easiest to see the reasoning behind this statement if we compare and contrast a few example situations. The situations have echoes in real life, but are not meant to reflect the situations in any specific organizations.

As you read the descriptions, you should consider three questions:

❏ What are the critical differences in the various situations?
❏ How might these differences affect how you would manage the change?
❏ Do any of them appear similar to change situations you have experienced? If not, jot down the specific circumstances of your experience so that you can draw your own conclusions as we explore the situations in more depth.

Situation 1: the lift company

Bill was the production manager of the main UK factory of a subsidiary of an international organization. His factory made lifts, the main items produced being lift machinery, lift cars, architectural items, such as landing door frames, and spares.

The factory had been laid out so that like machines were grouped in banks. A product moved across the factory floor with different people working on different stages. No one could easily identify where their work contributed to a particular job.

The white-collar employees who interfaced with the factory floor workers were aloof, and thought the factory workers were slackers, a feeling totally reciprocated by those on the factory floor. Union representatives were tough, but not unreasonable, and had agreed changes in the past when they were convinced that they were in the best interests of the firm and the workers.

Much of the product was made to supply marketing companies across the world, and to keep this business the factory had to be as effective as factories in Asia and other parts of Europe. In the past year, unit costs had become higher than those of other factories in the worldwide group. Bill had always had difficulty in meeting delivery dates, largely because the vast factory made it difficult to establish the point a contract had reached at any particular time. He knew it was late when it did not arrive at the other end. Quality was only maintained by means of an army of inspectors, with rejections adding to delay and costs. Unless things improved, he knew that the factory stood to lose a major part of its volume to other factories in the multinational group.

Bill's solution was to change the entire way in which things were done, grouping people around products rather than technologies, thereby creating what were really a series of semi-autonomous focused plants within the confines of the overall factory. Offices for the white-collar workers were to be built within the factory, with windows on all sides overlooking the factory floor. There was to be one such set of offices for each of the product areas, built within the 'territory' of the focused plant. A small team of two to three people was to be totally responsible for a particular product. A lift car, for example, would not then move around the factory but would be static, all work on building it being done by a small team, which would also be responsible for the quality of its own work.

Although people would work in different ways, be organized differently and need to be more flexible, none of the changes would be beyond the competence of the firm's employees. Bill did not envisage that there would be redundancies as the improved delivery performance and the reduction in costs brought about by the focused approach would bring more work into the plant, which would otherwise have gone to overseas factories. The threat of lost production would be averted.

Situation 2: the toiletries company

Jill is sales manager of a toiletries group. She had been a member of a project team looking at how to gain additional market share, and agreed with the conclusion that the company could obtain a significant increase by expanding distribution of the products. It had been concentrating on the larger chemists, departmental and variety stores. It needed to gain distribution in all the other outlets that sold its class of product.

The sales force had been divided into merchandisers and salespeople. Jill was certain that it would make sense to remove this specialization, reducing duplication of visits to outlets, and have all her team undertake both roles. This would free capacity to call on the other types of outlet.

Thus, part of the scheme that Jill wanted to set up involved visiting small chemists to take transfer orders that would be passed to the company via the wholesaler with whom the chemist normally dealt. The whole concept would mean changes to job roles, reallocation of sales territories and cause people to deal with types of outlet that were outside their present experience. Morale was not as high as she would have hoped, and the annual turnover of sales employees was higher than that of competitors. One of the reasons for this might have been that the company had grown very slowly over the past three years, an issue this new strategy would redress.

Situation 3: the newspaper company

The scene is a newspaper group in the early 1980s. Profits were falling towards danger level because of the ever-rising costs of producing newspapers. Technological developments had been made in the past ten years that could have reduced costs and given more flexibility, but the print workers and their union had kept a stranglehold on how newspapers were produced. They either refused to accept any changes or ensured that manning levels were kept at old levels, while wages rose because of the new skills.

New technology was now available that would cut out the need for many of the old processes, with journalists inputting their own stories into computer systems, which could be used more directly to make up the content of daily papers. Many of the old skills of the print workers were therefore redundant, and almost everyone in the company would have to operate differently. However, fear of strikes and sabotage – which would have been a consequence of any attempt to change without the agreement of the print workers – had held the company in check. However, at this point the managing director is being forced to act because the bottom-line position is deteriorating and a new company has entered the industry, producing newspapers using the new process and thereby gaining an immense competitive advantage.

Situation 4: the innovation

Harold is responsible for a small internal consultancy group of three people. The group has developed a new forecasting process that, studies have convinced the group, could have a positive effect on the whole company if it were to be adopted, reducing inventories and reducing delays in fulfilling orders. The concept is technical, but can be built into the marketing and manufacturing processes of the company without major disruption.

Harold believes that the risks are low, as other companies use something similar, although without the refinements and features of this approach. His department does not have the power to force such a change within the organization, but all the calculations point to the enormous benefit the company could gain by making this innovation.

Situation 5: the new manager

Anne has recently been appointed information manager in a large company. She had previously worked in the information department of a competitor. Her unit is small, consisting of four well-qualified professionals and a departmental secretary.

When Anne was interviewed, it was made clear that there was dissatisfaction with the role the unit had been playing, and that the company felt it was not getting the information it needed to help cope with all the changes going on around it.

The issue was seen as critical by top management, which was trying to follow a flexible approach in order to adapt quickly to the turbulence of the environment and markets. It become clear that there was some urgency regarding this issue and that if she succeeded in turning the unit around, she would have a good future, but if she failed there would be a reappraisal of her position after six months.

During her first few weeks in the new job, Anne carried out a quick survey of the way the unit was meeting the needs of the internal clients, examined the way the unit was organized and the overall procedures for obtaining, storing and retrieving information. As a result, she formed a number of ideas for improvement, which she wants to implement. Although none of these would affect the job security or salaries of her staff, it is possible that one or two of her colleagues might feel that the new approaches would reduce their status as 'expert' in a particular field. One man who would certainly feel this way resented that she had been appointed from outside, and believed that the job should have been given to him.

CRITICAL FACTORS THAT INFLUENCE THE CHOICE OF MANAGEMENT STYLE

By now you will have your own thoughts about the differences between these situations. Some critical factors that may affect which management style is seen to be most appropriate are listed below, and these will be used in our comparisons of the case situations with each other so we can be more precise about the differences between them. We can then examine what might be an appropriate style in each situation.

❏ *Is the change incremental or fundamental?*
An *incremental* change – which might be called more of the same – is rarely as threatening as a *fundamental* change, after which the organization may be very different in many ways. Incremental changes are often exciting for everyone, although they may pose threats to individuals when they are accompanied by a need to do a job differently. Fundamental change may be exciting for the few, but scary for the many, and may be psychologically threatening.

❏ *How urgent is the need for the change?*
When urgency is moderate or low, more time may be available for participation. When it is critical that the organization makes the change fast, the need to beat the enemy of time may mean that longer-term benefits that might have come from a more participative approach are simply impracticable. We should distinguish between *real* crisis and *manufactured* crisis – the latter occurring when a manager sets an unnecessarily short timescale for change, which is not justified by the situation.

❏ *What sort of impact will the change have on the organization?*
Changes may be big or small, and in crisis situations may even be of the 'bet the company' type. Often impact and urgency go hand in hand, but this is not inevitable. Something that will have a very high impact should receive even more careful attention with regard to the provision of resources and to the change management process than something that will have a minor impact.

❏ *How fierce is the internal resistance to change likely to be?*
Sometimes resistance can be reduced by the style of change management adopted, but there are other situations where no amount of participation will do this, and too much discussion can actually reinforce resistance. Chapter 4 deals with resistance in more depth.

❏ *Do those affected by the change have the ability to participate?*
We might add 'or can they acquire this ability'. In a sense, the degree of resistance may express the psychological willingness of employees to participate, whereas their skills and competencies are about their ability to relate to the change, and, through their understanding, contribute to it. This does not mean that there should be zero participation for those who do not seem able to contribute to the change process, but it does affect how and where they are asked to participate. There is, of course, a danger of underestimating people and this should be guarded against.

❏ *Will the change bring job losses?*
Today the answer is increasingly 'yes'. If a large number of

those in the organization will lose their jobs, this will affect the depth and breadth of participation.

❏ *Is the change restricted to one area of management responsibility?* If the change you are trying to manage will affect only your department, you can make straightforward choices, but often there are complications as many departments are affected.

The right solution emerges from a combination of answers rather than from any single answer. High resistance and low urgency may, for example, allow for a different style to be adopted than will high resistance and crisis. The choice of style should come from a consideration of all the factors together, plus some understanding of the relative importance of each.

Table 2.1 analyses the five situations outlined earlier against the critical factors listed above. You may care to extend this to cover any change situation that you might have been considering as you read this section.

WHAT IS THE RIGHT STYLE FOR A GIVEN SITUATION?

Remember, we are trying to choose the degree of participation that will be most effective in implementing the change. The inspiration for the classifications used comes from an article by D A Stace and D C Dunphy ('Translating Business Strategies into Action: Managing Strategic Change, *Strategic Change'*, 1 April 1992). The labels are descriptive enough to require little elaboration. They are:

❏ *collaborative* – let's work this out together;
❏ *consultative* – your views are important and I really do want your feedback;
❏ *directive* – this is what I want you to do;
❏ *coercive* – do this or take the consequences.

There are penalties for getting the style wrong. Some may be immediate, such as a failure of the initiative. Others may be longer-term, in that the change appears to have been effective, but at the cost of low morale, passive resistance, resignations that the organizations did not wish to take place and, occasionally, sabotage that continues long after the change has happened.

Eight generic positions are described below, with an indication of the style that appears to be most appropriate for each following. The positions use three of the classifications defined above: the nature of the change, its urgency, and the degree of resistance. The description under each heading shows how other factors mentioned above might influence the final choice. Reference will be made to the case situations, so that we can draw some conclusions about which is an appropriate style for each.

In all situations, change has to be led. The first four generic possibilities relate to incremental change, the second four to fundamental (or transformational) change. Two different strengths of resistance and urgency are considered in each case. This could be visualized as a pair of matrices, onto which the underlying analysis might be written.

Incremental change (more of the same)

Low urgency, low resistance

For this type of change and level of urgency and resistance, a collaborative approach is ideal. There is time to involve those affected by the change, which may lead to better ways of implementing it, and to higher motivation. At the same time, the widespread support for the change means that such participation should be effective. It is unlikely that this type of change will lead to job losses. The degree of collaboration might reduce somewhat if the employees involved lack the ability to make any sensible contribution. In some cases it may not be possible for the change leader to involve people in the actual decision (for exam-

Table 2.1 Analysis of five situations

Factor	Situation 1: the lift company	Situation 2: the toiletries company	Situation 3: the newspaper company	Situation 4: the innovation	Situation 5: the new manager
Type of change	Fundamental	Incremental	Fundamental	Incremental	Incremental
Urgency	High	Moderate	Crisis	Low	High
Results/impact	Very high	High	Extremely high	High	Could be high
Resistance	Not unreasonable	Low	Extremely high	Unknown	Mixed high and low
Employee capability	OK	Can relate to change	Perceived threats	May not understand the techniques	Employees capable
Impact on jobs	Improved security (avoids redundancy)	Growth opportunities	Redundancies: threats and opportunities	No disruption	Threat to status, not to employment
Areas of responsibility affected	All within the factory	Only those initiating the change	Whole organization	Many departments	Own department

ple it may be imposed from elsewhere in the organization), but it is usually desirable to ensure that everyone knows the reasons for the change, and involvement may focus on how to implement it.

Situation 4, the innovation problem, is likely to be in this category, and the need for collaboration is increased because the innovation will only take place if it can gain widespread support from the other departments where the change will take place. There is a need in this case to develop an understanding of the new techniques among key people in those departments, so that they can be fully involved in the change. Support from other managers is only likely if they come to believe in the change.

High urgency, low resistance

In this case, time is not on our side, unless the number of people who are affected is small. This may force a mix of collaboration and consultation, where the former is focused on fewer key people, and the latter gives the majority an opportunity to give feedback but means that they are less involved in determining how to make the change work.

This probably reflects most closely the position in situation 2, the toiletries company (although there the urgency was only moderate). In this, situation the change would be contained within the marketing and sales departments, with sales being affected the most. Jill would need to give some thought to whether or not she could use this change situation to build more stability in the sales force, and should ensure that everyone is given whatever coaching or training support is needed to develop necessary new skills. If the vision behind the strategy can be shared by those affected, most will also see personal benefits arising from the changes.

Low urgency, high resistance

Time is available, so it may be possible to use a collaborative style, but this degree of resistance means that it must also be persuasive to try to increase the level of support.

In such an incremental change situation, where people's jobs may not be threatened, it may be possible to demonstrate that the change benefits the individual as well as the organization. This is much harder to do, indeed, it may be impossible, on a widespread basis if redundancies are involved. A lot depends on the number of people affected by the change, and the probability is that the manager should use a somewhat different style for different groups, perhaps using a collaborative style with those who are needed to help implement the change, and a consultative style with others. If resistance cannot be overcome, the manager may have to be more directive with some people. None of our five situations mirrors this scenario.

High urgency, high resistance

In this situation, there may be a need to balance the benefits of persuasive consultation against the need for a more directive approach with persuasive undertones. In cases of extreme urgency and extreme resistance, the only solution is to be coercive, but this style should be used only as a last resort.

Situation 5, the new manager, is interesting because there is a mix of high and low resistance. The numbers of people involved are small, which makes it easier to try a collaborative style, which would be right for the low resisters, and there is a good chance that this could work. However, it looks as if Anne might have an underlying problem to deal with in the disgruntled manager, even though his attitude has little to do with the change itself. If she had been managing a very large unit in the organization, employing hundreds of people, many of whom were incapable of aiding the change, she might have been forced to be more directive, as suggested above. Fortunately, however, she has the opportunity to work with people in groups and on a one-to-one basis. Also, she knows that they all have the ability to help make the change a success, if only they all have the willingness. In her situation, attention to ways of reducing resistance might pay dividends.

Transformational (or fundamental) change

The degree of urgency cannot be low in this case as there is little point in making a fundamental change if it does not appear to be needed. The extremes examined here are therefore 'high' and 'crisis'. Resistance is 'high' or 'low', as with incremental change. In all fundamental change situations the style required has to have a strong visionary element on top of the involvement dimension. This will be discussed in detail at a later stage.

Low resistance, high urgency

Involvement is still appropriate, although it may vary between collaboration with key people to consultation and informing others. The visionary element is important, and a charismatic leadership style will often work well here. Because resistance is low, people are willing to follow the lead of someone they trust and who inspires them.

In situation 1, the lift company, resistance is potentially more than low, but past experience is that a good argument will be accepted. There are no job losses envisaged and, in fact, the actions should secure jobs and create new opportunities, and Bill's intentions do not go beyond the abilities of those he intends to lead into the change. Of course, all departments at the factory will be affected, and there will be implications for many other areas of the organization, all of which should be beneficial. We will use this situation in the next chapter to examine in more detail how Bill might assess the implications of this very complicated change situation.

Low resistance, crisis situation

This is more difficult. Again, the visionary element is important in helping the people see how the organization can come out of the crisis, but collaboration will be restricted to a few key people. Widespread communication is important, telling it how it is, but so is persuading people that the changes will solve the crisis.

There may be a need to lean towards a directive approach.

Where the crisis is both real and widely understood, and particularly if it threatens the survival of the organization, a directive approach is often acceptable, even though the same people might resent such an approach if there were no crisis: people look for strong leadership in a crisis situation.

High resistance, high urgency

The judgement is whether or not persuasive or consultative approaches can reduce the level of resistance fast enough to allow the changes to be implemented. The chances of success are influenced by the numbers of people involved, the perceived importance of the move to the organization and the scale of any job losses. The visionary element is important, but the style for all except the top team may have to be directive and sometimes even coercive because the change must take place quickly. A sound communication strategy, to explain to and inform people about what is going on, will be needed.

High resistance, crisis situation

A visionary dictator may offer the only solution to making the changes in time!

However, in this position, very careful thought should be given to managing the survivors of the change, as people may then need a much more supportive style. It may be possible to be less coercive if there is a good chance of winning people over to the change and lowering resistance.

In situation 3, the newspaper company, it is a reasonable assumption that the resistance by the print workers will not fall away if persuasion is used. In any case, large numbers of them would not be required and others would have to be retrained, so the company has less to lose if they all go out on strike, as this would give an opportunity to recruit new people to do the different jobs that the company now requires. The company has everything to lose if it continues in the old way, and everything to gain by change.

In this situation, it is difficult to see how anything but a coercive approach could work. The managing director should think carefully about all the possible outcomes of such a confrontational approach, although there is little choice if a change is to be made in the circumstances described.

However, even in this situation, it should be possible to use a less extreme style in those areas of the company where resistance is lower: the situation describes the print workers, but not other groups, such as the journalists, who may have different feelings.

Selecting the appropriate style is not a dogmatic exercise, and there are other factors that may affect what is possible. In situations of low morale and motivation, a judgement has to be made about whether or nor involvement will improve morale or just reinforce the negative feelings. Similarly, the culture of the organization may force a move to a lower level of involvement, simply because to behave differently would be viewed with suspicion. The level of involvement may have to be reduced when the issue is highly confidential. In all situations, however, it is important to consider the effect that the chosen style will have on the longer-term, post-change situation so that appropriate strategies can be put in place ready for when the change has been implemented.

In the above discussion, references were made to a visionary approach, to communication and to actions such as training that might facilitate change in a particular situation. Although these references helped to make some sense of the example situations, they were not put together in an overall context. Before we move on to detailed examination, we should define the broad steps that are required to ensure an effective change management situation:

❑ *Assess the implications of the proposed change*
  The chances of success are greatly increased when the overall impact of the change is understood. This is a matter for detailed analysis, not broad brush thinking, and such analysis will often reveal implications that had not previously

been considered. For example, you will need to think about what will help or hinder the change and what should be done about it.

❑ *Manage the change process*
A six-stage approach is suggested, which will later be refined to give the EASIER model. The approach gives weight to both the behavioural and analytical aspects. In broad terms, the six steps are:

1. establish a vision for the outcome of the change;
2. gain a shared commitment to this vision;
3. give support to those involved in the change;
4. make detailed plans for the change;
5. monitor progress in implementing the change;
6. recognize the role others have played in making the change happen.

❑ *Know when to declare a halt to the change process*
This may look like a silly point at first sight, but, in fact, it is important. This is because change sometimes fails when the wrong stopping point is chosen. Delayering of an organization is not implemented at the point where a new organogram is published and those declared redundant have left. Rather, it is only implemented when it is working smoothly and effectively, which may be many months later. Many of the failures mentioned in Chapter 1 might have been caused by choosing a premature stopping point for the change process.

The next chapter will begin the process of making sense of the various stages of this approach.

3

ASSESSING THE IMPLICATIONS OF A CHANGE MANAGEMENT SITUATION

A prerequisite for the management of any change is a full understanding of what is proposed and its implications. This may sound an empty truism, but there are notable examples that emphasize the point. In the UK the words 'poll tax' and 'Child Protection Agency' conjure up images of major changes that were somewhat less effective than intended because many of the implications – visible to the man in the street with a normal allotment of common sense but not to their devisors – were not thought through in advance. The whole of Europe must have looked on in astonishment at the numerous ineffective changes announced by the British government or the European Commissioners over the BSE crisis over British cattle. Many must feel that the whole crisis could have been avoided had the issue been properly thought through when the first signs of the disease became known in the 1980s.

This book is not covering anything as breathtaking as national change, but even on a more modest scale, every change manager should face up to the issue of what the change itself means, followed by its interrelationship with the various elements that make up the organization. The first part of this chapter deals with these matters.

There is another type of early planning that will also aid the change management process. The wise manager will give some thought to the factors in their situation that either help or hinder the implementation of the change, both with a view to trying to improve the odds in favour of the change and to helping them select the most appropriate style with which to manage the implementation of that change. A way of aiding thought about this will be offered in the last part of this chapter.

ANALYSING THE CHANGE

Figure 3.1 illustrates a way of thinking through the implications of a change. The lines emphasize that no part of this diagram exists in a vacuum, and a change to any one of the variables may affect any or all of the others. The variable at the top of the figure is our change decision, and the others represent various dimensions of the integrated organization. Ideally, the change we want should drive what happens in the other variables: in practice, this will only happen if specific attention is given to it.

What is going on with any of the variables could affect the ability of a manager to manage a change effectively. Imagine that you are implementing a change, a key platform of which is team-working and setting and meeting team targets. Your task might become impossible if, at the same time, the human resources department changed the bonus system to one that emphasized individual effort. Either your change will fail or the bonus scheme has to be changed to emphasize what you want to do.

In any change situation, there are things that are obvious and others that may be hidden. If a decision to downsize will lead to the redundancy of 10 per cent of the organization's employees, it is an immediate conclusion that action has to be taken to set a fair redundancy programme that meets the requirements of employment law. But there is also a less obvious and more difficult aspect to consider. If 10 per cent of employees leave the organization, how will this affect the jobs of the remaining 90 per cent? If layers of middle managers are removed, can we assume that those at the top and bottom of the organization can continue to manage and be managed in exactly the manner as in the past? It is usually these more hidden things that tend to be overlooked, although the success or otherwise of the change may depend on them.

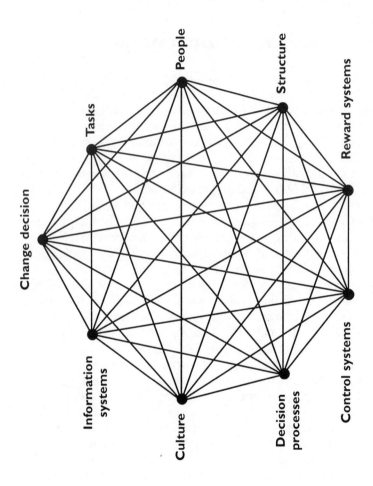

Figure 3.1 *An integrated view of an organization*

We shall now describe the variables shown in Figure 3.1 with a list of some of the factors that should be considered for each one. This is followed by an analysis of situation 1, the lift company, to show how the approach works in practice.

Change decision

What is the change that is to be made, and what is involved in implementing it? The questions raised in trying to answer this question, listed below, can only be indicative because there are many different types of change. Use them to help you generate a list of what is important in your own change situation:

❑ What is the change?
❑ What are the reasons for the change?
❑ What are the implications for customers?
❑ Does it require any physical changes to buildings, plant layout, etc?
❑ Does it require new investment?
❑ What disruption is likely during the change period?
❑ How long will the change take to implement?
❑ Which departments of the organization will be directly affected?
❑ Which will be indirectly affected?
❑ What are the risks of the change?

Tasks

These are the things that the organization has to do in order to make the change and operate under the new conditions. It includes the non-repetitive tasks required to handle the change itself and, as importantly, the new tasks that have to be undertaken continuously under the changed conditions.

❑ What new tasks will the organization have to undertake as a result of the change?
❑ What existing tasks will have to be done in a totally different way?

❏ What existing tasks will have to be undertaken in a different place?
❏ What new priorities are there for the tasks the organization has to undertake?
❏ Which of the tasks have to be undertaken within the organization, and which could equally well be contracted out or done by other means?

People

The analysis so far shows what has to be done. The next step is to look at the implications in terms of our human resources.

❏ Do we have people who have the skills and competencies required by the new situation?
❏ Are they available in the right numbers?
❏ Do we have to train or coach people so that they can be effective in the new situation?
❏ If we have to recruit, how easy will it be to find people with the right skills and competencies?
❏ Are the skills and competencies we have at the location where they will be needed?
❏ Will the change cause redundancies?
❏ Are people likely to lose their jobs because they do not have the ability to acquire the new skills or change their old attitudes?
❏ Will the changes be seen as a breach of the psychological contract (see Chapter 4) by any individuals?
❏ Do we need to look more closely at the potential effect on key individuals or different classes of employee?

Structure

This is the way tasks are grouped into jobs, and jobs into reporting relationships.

❏ Do we need to change existing organizational units to enable the change to take place?

❏ Do we need to add new activity areas to the structure?
❏ Should reporting relationships be altered?
❏ If changes are not made to the structure, will it be possible to implement the planned decision?
❏ Are there any changes needed to the geographical location of any elements of the structure?
❏ Do people have to be managed differently as a consequence of the change?

Reward systems

It should not be assumed that existing reward systems will match the new situation. The reward system and the objective of the change must be aligned. It is unlikely that there will be one answer to each question, and each category of employee may need to be examined separately. The reward system for sales-people may be fine, for example, while that for managers may drive behaviour in the wrong direction.

❏ Which desired behaviours are stimulated by present monetary reward systems?
❏ Which are impeded by the monetary reward systems?
❏ Which are neutral?
❏ Would change to the monetary reward system enable the change to be implemented more easily?
❏ Will the change we are implementing cause anyone to lose pay? (For example, a change in sales territories could mean that some people's take-home pay is reduced.)
❏ Will the change cause anyone to gain additional rewards that are not deserved?
❏ Do we have too many grade and pay scale variations for the new structure?
❏ Are promotional prospects enhanced or diminished by the proposed change?
❏ How will non-monetary rewards be affected by the change?

Control systems

The way in which the organization exercises control may also be inappropriate for the new situation. For example, if the aim of a change is to establish a long-term position, it is pointless to continue with a control system that only measures short-term results.

❑ Is the management control system adequate to monitor the implementation of the change?
❑ Is the management control system appropriate for the position we want to be in after the change?
❑ Are short-term results linked to the longer-term position we are trying to achieve by means of the change?
❑ Is the management control system timely enough for what we need to monitor?
❑ Does it report with adequate frequency?
❑ Does the performance management system encourage the behaviours that will be needed after the change?
❑ Are there other control systems that should be examined because they are relevant to the change? (Such as production control, complaints.)
❑ Are there any aspects of the control systems that could damage the implementation of the change because they drive behaviour in the wrong way?

Decision processes

This variable covers both the decision-making process and who is empowered to make decisions.

The way in which decisions are reached often has to respond to the new shape and direction of the organization. For example, a delayered organization cannot function effectively unless there is clarity about empowerment (and this takes us back to how tasks will change and then to whether or not the people possess the competencies to enable empowerment to work).

❑ Does the change require any alteration to who is empowered to make critical decisions?

❏ Is the current procedure for making major decisions timely enough for the changed situation?
❏ What changes should be made to the procedures in place in the organization?
❏ Who will have perceived powers reduced by the change?
❏ Who will have perceived powers increased by the change?

Culture

Does the culture of the organization support or retard the intended change?

❏ Does our culture encourage the behaviours that we need as a result of the change?
❏ Does it discourage what we want to achieve?
❏ Will it prevent the change from succeeding?
❏ Will the change bring adverse consequences to the culture?
❏ If we need to deliberately change the culture to fit a new situation, do we really understand what is involved?

Information systems

Information is part of the lifeblood that makes the body corporate function. Any change can bring with it a need to review the information system in terms of what is collected, how it is aggregated and to whom it is disseminated.

❏ Is the right information being collected, stored and retrieved?
❏ Do we need to put more resources into the information system to meet the changes?
❏ Are we collecting information that will become irrelevant after the change?
❏ Are the right people receiving the information?

This gives us enough to provoke thought. Of course some changes will not bring with them a need to alter these variables, and very few changes will mean altering every variable. It is also unlikely that many managers can answer all the questions posed without assistance or, indeed, other questions that will emerge as specific to a particular change situation. It is often an ideal opportunity to use a working party of people with specialist knowledge to work on all the issues. This also has the advantage that if the decision is then made to proceed with the change, the process of involvement has already started. Although the ideal is for this work to be started before the change is underway, it is not necessary to be dogmatic. In some situations, such an analysis may be broadened to include many who are key to the change, and be the basis of one of the first workshops that are intended to create a shared vision. It is also possible to use other people to help assess the implications of the change, in a totally directive manner, calling for reports and figures, for example, without allowing them to participate in the overall process.

THE LIFT COMPANY REVISITED

Lists of headings are useful when you are faced with the need to apply yourself to a problem, but they may make for boring reading, which can defeat understanding. A worked example is often more helpful. The fundamental change situation faced by the lift company has been chosen for this purpose here because it causes more impact on all the variables than the other examples we looked at earlier and is therefore best for illustration. The story is continued below, tracing some of the paths that Bill began to follow as he thought through the implications of his bright idea.

Situation 1, part 2: the lift company

Bill had six senior managers reporting to him: manufacturing, warehousing, purchasing, facilities, personnel, and accounting.

We join him at the stage where he had a broad vision of what he wanted to achieve, but needed to do more to ensure that all aspects of the change were understood before he went much further.

Bill believed that his top management team should be involved in this major change from the outset because if it did not share his vision, there would be little hope of gaining commitment at lower levels. He had talked individually to everyone about his idea, and decided that the best way to move towards the next step would be to get the whole top team to collaborate in assessing the implications and, ultimately, what would have to be done about them. This would give him confidence that nothing was overlooked and stress the importance he placed on their experience and judgement.

All were sworn to secrecy as everyone agreed that premature leaking of the idea could frustrate the change.

At the first meeting, the initial discussion was about the threat the factory faced and the possibilities offered by the focused approach. Bill was satisfied that everyone was at least open-minded, even though his own very strong enthusiasm was not yet shared by them all. He stressed that if they followed his vision and the change failed to achieve the results, they would not get another chance. However, if they did nothing, the factory was certain to lose most of its volume and his expectation was that it would close. So, unless anyone had a better idea for correcting the situation, the firm would not be worse off after the changes and had a very good chance of succeeding.

Using a checklist based on the integrated organization model (see Figure 3.1), they began to assess what the likely implications of the change would be. Bill had set up some large whiteboards on which he had ruled three columns headed 'issue', 'variables impacted', and 'notes' – the aim being to consider the issues under the headings of the model. The middle column was to prevent everyone from bouncing all the way round the model for every issue, while ensuring that none of the important connections were forgotten.

They began to discuss the 'change decision' itself and rapidly produced a list of issues that filled one of the whiteboards. There was some debate about the number of focused units that should be set up, the numerous changes to the layout of the factory floor, how the offices could be fitted in without causing any hazards, whether or not the changes would result in more or less floor space being needed, whether or not some of the machinery should be changed and what the costs might be. Also, in an operating plant, such major changes could not be made without closing the factory for a spell, and there was much debate about how long it would take to change things round and whether or not it could be done during the annual shutdown, which would take place in the summer. Many similar issues went down on the checklists. Although people occasionally made remarks like 'would the lads agree to this', the middle column was almost empty. The final column was so full that everything had to be written in abbreviations.

This changed when they moved to the 'tasks' variable. The manufacturing manager led by saying nothing much would change, as lifts still had to be produced, but he was immediately challenged by the others. As they talked, they realized that there would need to be a more empowered manager in charge of each unit, that the quality inspection task would change to TQM, that although the skills needed to manufacture the lifts were the same, individuals would have to be more flexible in what they did, and so the list built up. The centre column began to be filled with cross-references to culture, people, structure, information systems and control systems.

Under the 'people' heading the first concern was whether or not everyone was capable of making the changes, and what would happen to them if they could not. The need to provide training in various areas was a main topic. Despite the middle column, there were many murmurings about whether or not the culture would prevent the changes from happening. It was agreed that the changes would not reduce the numbers of employees needed, and that if there were people who could not cope with the changes to their roles, the organization should be big enough to be able to allocate them to other tasks without loss of status.

It was agreed that each manager should work with the personnel department to identify individuals who might find it difficult to adapt. The personnel managers raised queries about how the white-collar workers would feel about being put in the factory, and it was agreed that much needed to be thought through to make this an attractive and acceptable matter. Gradually, this whiteboard also filled up, and the cross-reference column had entries for almost every issue.

The discussion took in every box in the model shown in Figure 3.1, although what arose in consideration of the later boxes often sent the team back to think further about issues they thought they had covered. By the end of the day, team members had thought thoroughly about the obvious and subtle changes that needed to be made to the structure and satisfied themselves that where a job disappeared, it was replaced by another of equal or higher standing.

The discussion about reward systems revealed that the present number of bands impaired flexibility and that much of the grading/pay structure should be modified. The question of team bonuses for the various units was raised as a possibility.

Numerous changes to the control systems were identified, varying from management reporting to costing systems to production control. It was agreed that information would have to flow differently to match the new structure and tasks. Decisions would be taken at different points in the organization, and all workers would have a higher degree of empowerment (which took them back to the 'people' issues once more and whether or not anyone would feel that they had lost influence as a result of the changes).

Finally, they reached 'culture'. They accepted that the physical changes would help a culture shift, but that much would have to be done to achieve the degree of flexibility and teamwork that was needed. Brainstorming ideas included putting a meeting room in each unit's office, to make it easier for the supervisors, technicians and white-collar workers to get together for regular, short meetings, equipping every unit with different colour overalls, and ensuring that the training given supported the new culture. Another idea was that if people could identify with a particular contract, and feel pride in it, it should be possible to follow the prestige contracts through and take videos of them in operation after installation, showing how they enhanced the buildings in which they were installed. They went back to systems again as there was a realization that the performance management systems should change to reflect the culture they were seeking. There was a recognition that the information systems needed to give more feedback to the shop floor, so that each unit felt part of the success or failure of the operation, and that this would require a coherent briefing process down the line.

At the conclusion of this meeting, those present knew they had a great deal of further work to do, just to establish the implications of the change, but they also realized that they had also taken the first steps towards planning the change. Everyone felt more convinced that, despite all the work involved, the new concept would have a good chance of delivering what was expected from it. Some of the gloom that they had felt settling on them over the past few months began to dissipate as they felt that perhaps their future might, after all, still be under their control.

Comment on the lift company's situation

What I hope you can see from the above description is how changes in the variables may also cause other variables to change. It should be no surprise that an organization could think easily about the physical, cost and production implications of such a change, punctuated by occasional references to industrial relations. Unfortunately, managers in change situations do not always probe deeper than this. Some structural changes are always self-evident. If new units are being set up, say, it is obvious that people have to be grouped differently, but, as the example shows, there are many, many more issues that have to be dealt with to ensure success, and many of these are *not* obvious unless they are sought out. In time, many would emerge as the change progressed, but might by then have prevented it from achieving its desired results or the variable might have become harder to alter.

In the case of the lift company, it is clearly better to anticipate problems, and deal with as many as possible in one overall change, than to tackle them in dribs and drabs. The importance of the change and its fundamental nature mean that there may not be a second chance if the change fails. Everything humanly possible must be done to make it work.

Not all change situations are like this and, in reality, not all managers will be able to change all the variables we have just discussed. Jill, in the toiletries company situation described in the last chapter, runs an integrated department, few if any of the jobs being duplicated elsewhere in the organization. It is easy to see that she, for example, could have a bonus system changed as only her people would be affected. However, Anne, the new manager, only has five people in her unit, so, even if she finds the bonus system counterproductive, there may be 995 other people in the company at the same grades whose managers believe that the current system suits their purposes very well.

Being realistic about where changes to the variables can be made does not negate the value of identifying the ideal situation. Working in full knowledge of the difficulties is always better than acting in ignorance and making poor decisions when things do not work out as well as hoped. If there is an obstacle that you cannot shift, it may be possible to go round it. If the natural tendency of a reward system is to drive people away from the behaviour you want, maybe you can compensate for this in the criteria you use in the performance management system, by providing more coaching than you would otherwise need to or by setting up something else to help compensate something that for you is a given. Finally, remember the story of the last straw. It may be that your discussion with those who can authorize removal of the thing that blocks is the latest of many complaints raised by managers elsewhere, and may be enough to get things moving.

ASSESSING THE PROSPECTS FOR SUCCESSFUL CHANGE

In any change situation, even ones that are not complicated, it is worth while to think through what might prevent the change and what might help it. One approach that is often useful is equilibrium analysis, which is a form of force field analysis. Imagine a pad inside a cylinder. It moves up the cylinder by means of air pressure from below and, if there were no counterforces, would pop out of the top. However, weights are added to the pad that hold it down. Greater air pressure makes it rise more, additional weights push it down. If we transfer this image to the management situation, we can think of the air pressure as the series of circumstances and actions that cause something to be as good as it is and the weights as the series of circumstances and actions that stop it from being better and are trying to make it worse than it is. 'Trying' may be an exaggeration sometimes because there may be no intent, but, nevertheless, the force exercised is negative.

Figure 3.2 develops this idea into a simple technique. The line across the page is the situation. The line to the side is a scale that we can use to assess the severity of each factor identified relative to the other factors. To explore this we need a new character and situation. The figure represents Richard's assessment of why the meeting he runs with his team every month does not seem to deliver many results. The horizontal line represents the state of effectiveness of the meeting: he cannot define this precisely, but he knows it is not very effective. The arrows under the line are why it is not worse than it is, while those above the line show why it is as bad as it is. The lengths of the arrows show the importance Richard places on each of the factors.

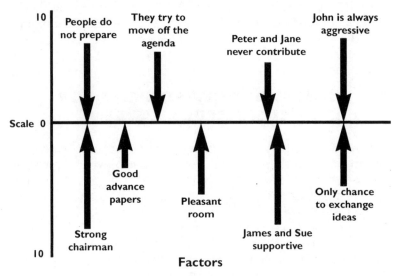

Figure 3.2 *Why is the monthly management meeting not more effective?*

When you look at a diagram like this, you see that performance could be improved by increasing some of the positive forces. Alternatively, the meeting might be more effective if some negative factors were removed or reduced. This second option may be better because it may be easier than the first and sometimes increasing the positive force may cause an increase in a negative one. An example of this is that Richard thinks he is a strong chairman (he may be wrong!) Coming on even stronger might well cause John to respond even more aggressively, so that what is gained by Richard's efforts is lost by John's response.

The meeting situation was chosen because we have all experienced meetings of one sort or another that did not seem to achieve very much, and everyone can fill in this figure for themselves, substituting factors from personal experience and removing those that do not fit.

That is the technique. Now that it is clear what you have to do, let us apply it to what might be the case in one of the situations we looked at in the previous chapter. I have chosen Harold and his innovation, and a possible result is shown in Figure 3.3.

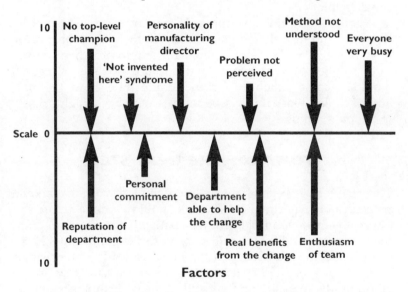

Figure 3.3 *What helps or hinders the innovation situation*

Harold's situation is typical of many where the manager trying to lead the change does not have authority over all the areas of the organization that have to implement it. The figure shows the assessment that Harold might make of the situation. It is possible to see that there is little he could do to increase the positive forces. Neither the reputation of the department nor the enthusiasm of his team can be increased in the short term, and the benefits of the change can not be increased if everything is worked out properly in the first place.

Of the six hindering forces, there are three that might be addressed, while the issue of the personality of the manufacturing director may affect how Harold tries to implement the innovation. It could make sense to find a champion for the idea very quickly, someone with more power than he has, who will support and promote the innovation. It could be the director to whom he reports, the managing director or perhaps the marketing director.

When seeking this champion, Harold needs first to concentrate on building a shared perception that there is a problem. No busy manager will give him much air time to present a complicated solution to what is thought to be a non-existent problem. It would become much easier to demonstrate how the new approach will work if the issue it deals with has a high priority in people's minds.

TOWARDS THE NEXT STEP

This chapter has been about the pre-planning work that should precede a change situation. Thus, it should be done before any attempt is made to implement the change. The amount of effort that these steps will take will vary with the complexity of the change and the knowledge of the manager leading the change. As we have seen, it does not have to be an exercise done in isolation by the manager and, indeed, in really complicated situations it is unlikely that any one person will have all the knowledge needed to make the assessment in this way.

We are almost ready to move on to the next stage of our change approach – the application of the EASIER model – but before we do this we should give attention to one more area: the problem of resistance to change. This is the subject of the next chapter.

4

DEALING WITH RESISTANCE AND SURVIVOR ISSUES

In Chapter 2, it was shown how the strength of resistance to a change is one of the factors that affects the style of change management. While it is easy to see that the print workers in the newspaper situation would be totally hostile, because of the experience of many years, it is much more difficult to gauge where resistance will occur in many other change situations. Common sense tells us that if there are to be massive redundancies, very few people will be jumping for joy, but there are numerous situations where the factors causing resistance are more subtle. One of the aims of this chapter is to examine such causes in more detail. This is partly to enable a more accurate assessment to be made of the nature and strength of any resistance to change, partly because it may lead to ways of reducing this resistance during the change management process and partly because it may help the change manager to avoid initiating actions during the process that would cause resistance. By 'avoid', I mean seeking different ways to achieve the same ends, not giving up on something that should be done.

The second aim of this chapter is to give some thought to the motivational issues for survivors of a fundamental change that has led to colleagues losing their jobs. Not all changes create such situations, but when they do occur it is wise to give such issues serious attention. It can be harmful to the change to assume that all the survivors will breathe a collective sigh of relief at keeping their jobs and then feel and behave as if nothing had happened. So, although the situation may not occur in the changes managed by everyone, there will be some who will be involved in just such a problem.

RESISTANCE TO CHANGE

The history of mankind is of a journey of adaptation and change, which is one reason for the success of the human race. Of course, our ability to adapt and to instigate change comes partly from physical characteristics, such as having a well-developed brain and dextrous limbs, our ability to talk and the creative elements in our make-up that enable us both to develop new things and to visualize in advance how they will work.

So, it would be wrong to think that every change will cause rebellion and resistance. Change can be stimulating, and this is usually the case with incremental change, where growth and a feeling of natural progression may offer prospects for career development and an evolution of an individual's job. Thus, it would have come as no surprise to find that there were few problems of resistance in the toiletries company's situation of Chapter 2.

Resistance emerges when there is a threat to something the individual values. The threat may be real or it may be no more than a perception. It may arise from a genuine understanding of the change or from almost total ignorance about it. It may be something that the individual has thought about deeply or it may be just a feeling that the current state is very pleasant, so any proposal to alter it is a threat.

It would be very easy if, in every change situation, the threat could be overcome by showing how the individual will benefit. Unfortunately, this is not always possible, and in some circumstances can strike the individual as double-dealing if it is attempted. Talk about there being career opportunities elsewhere, for example, falls a bit flat when the individual's concern is losing their job and not being able to meet the mortgage repayments.

Threats

Threats come in all shapes and sizes, and to understand them it is necessary to look at them from the viewpoint of the individual. The manager leading the change has a different perspective, is in control of the change and has more knowledge about it than anyone else. Often the manager may be the only person who has reasonable certainty of passing through the turmoil of the change and coming out the other side intact.

In order to help develop this ability to consider things from another person's point of view, it is useful to consider the various ways in which change can threaten and why the same event may be looked at differently by different people. First, we will use Maslow's hierarchy of motivation as a means of measuring how threatening changes might be perceived to be. This will be followed by a consideration of the idea of the 'psychological contract', which helps us to explain why things that seem on the surface to pose no threat to a person may lead to uncompromising resistance. Not all resistance arises from fears, however, so we will also be consider some of the other causes.

Maslow's hierarchy of motivation

Maslow's argument is that there is a hierarchy of motivation, starting at the lowest level with basic needs for food, shelter and warmth, and progressing through various levels to self-fulfilment (self-actualization). Humans seek satisfaction of the level they are on and continually strive to move on to a higher level. The other needs do not disappear, but they are not motivators as long as they continue to be satisfied. When things start to collapse, the whole hierarchy may fall down. In Victorian times, loss of a job could mean near starvation for the person concerned, while modern Western society provides some safety net, but only at the most basic level. It therefore does not take much imagination to see how loss of a job can threaten not only self-fulfilment, achieved via excitement, responsibility and creativity, but every other level, down to and including the need for security. Not every person satisfies every level of need via the workplace. Table 4.1 shows how a selection of real or perceived threats may cause people to resist a change in order to protect their own positions.

The example is more clear cut than reality as actual human motivation may be much more complicated than this. Also, the patterns shown will not be the same for everyone and individual situations will vary, as will the personalities, hopes and aspirations of each person. So, the crosses in the table should be seen as an indication of what the effect *might* be, rather than a forecast of what it *will* be. The number of crosses against each level of motivation is a rough indication of the impact that might be expected, with one cross meaning the impact would be slight to three crosses meaning the impact would be great.

It should also be remembered that, according to Maslow's theory, a higher level of motivation cannot be adequately fulfilled while a lower level is unsatisfied. So, to return to the example of loss of a person's job, the longer-term impact on levels 3 and above may be much greater if the person cannot find a replacement job. However, this aspect of the theory need not concern us here as we are focusing on what may cause resistance, not on what happens to casualties of the change after they have left the organization. Also, it is the *perception* of the threat that motivates, even when no threat actually exists.

It does not require much imagination to think about what the threat of job loss means, and very few people would need Table 4.1 to make them realize that such a threat would cause a reaction. However, the majority of change situations do not have such drastic results. Many can create one or more of the other fears listed, but these may be harder to envisage. This is when we can use Maslow's hierarchy to act as a checklist, helping us think through where resistance might occur, ideally on an individual basis or, where this is not possible, for groups of people.

Table 4.1 *Threats from change to individual motivation*

Threats	Maslow's hierarchy of motivation				
	1. Basic	2. Security	3. Belonging	4. Prestige	5. Self-fulfilment
Loss of job	✕	✕✕✕	✕✕	✕✕	✕
Reduction of prospects				✕✕	✕
Fear of inability to do new job				✕	✕✕
Loss of current work group			✕✕		
Loss of authority		✕✕		✕✕	✕
Uncertainty about future			✕		

The 'psychological contract'

Another way of putting yourself in the position of the people affected by the change is to use the concept of the 'psychological contract'. There is more to every job than the written contractual terms, and it is this extra element that is the basis of the concept. The psychological contract is:

❏ unwritten;
❏ may be largely hidden, in that an individual may find it hard to articulate the 'terms' until they are threatened;
❏ may be more important to the person than the written contract;
❏ because of this, a breach may cause more resentment than anything affecting the written contract;
❏ the change manager may be in total ignorance of the expectations of the person, which makes a breach much more likely to occur.
❏ Two examples may make this clear. The first is very obvious, the second somewhat less so.

Example 1: the chief executive

Gerald is managing director of a global mining company. It is successful and he enjoys all the trappings of success – high salary, bonus schemes and a prestige car. The decisions he makes are far-reaching ones. Major investments and other strategic decisions are made by the board of which he is a member, but his recommendations normally go through as his colleagues know the thoroughness with which things are investigated and have great trust in his judgement. He has regular high-level contacts with governments in various countries, is frequently wooed by merchant bankers and is consulted on a number of matters by departments of the British government. Journalists interview him several times a year.

His company is taken over by a large conglomerate. He was opposed to the takeover, but the shareholders were convinced it was a good move. In fact, Gerald seems to have come out very well as his reward package has been increased and on paper he has the same responsibilities as before. He soon becomes dissatisfied, however. His investment decisions now need the approval of the parent board, of which he is not a member, compete with other requests from around the whole organization and are often rejected or deferred. As he no longer arranges the finance for his company, the bankers now ignore him. Governments tend to deal now with the main board director responsible for minerals and journalists no longer clamour for his attention.

In this situation, it is easy to see that large elements of what were important to Gerald about his job have disappeared. Very few of these would have found their way into his formal contract: it is the psychological contract that has changed. Although he thought he had opposed the takeover in the interests of the shareholders, it is impossible to say how much of his resistance was caused by a realization that his job would not in future carry the same prestige and excitement as it had hitherto.

Example 2: the accounting clerk

Kevin had worked for his company for ten years. He liked his job and knew that he could do it well, but he was not ambitious and did not really want to do anything else. Much of the work of the department was not open to him anyway, because he had no formal qualifications. He had a good relationship with his supervisor, who valued his opinions and had complete trust in the accuracy of his work. Because Kevin was naturally good with numbers, he was often asked to check the calculations of more senior, qualified members of the department. He felt that he was better than any computer, although he had never used one himself. Above all, Kevin valued the comradeship of the small unit in which he worked. He occasionally had to work late at regular busy times, such as the year end, but, for most of the year, knew that he would leave the office by 5.30pm and be home by 6.00. This was important to him, as it gave him time for a social life (he is unmarried) and enabled him to participate in his local amateur dramatic society, which was where he felt he could use all his talents.

One morning, the manager of the department called everyone together and said that there was to be a reorganization. Four people had recently left of their own accord and three others were due to retire in the next two months. None of these would be replaced. No one would be sacked, but the reduction in numbers coinciding with the expansion of the business meant that the remaining members of the department would have to cope with about a fifth more work than they were currently doing. In order to do this, the whole structure was being changed, and many people would find that they were expected to do either more or different tasks, that they were placed in different work groups and might find that they reported to a different supervisor. Additional computers were being made available to reduce the clerical burden and, of course, training would be given. However, it was inevitable that everyone would have to put in some extra time in order to keep the work flowing. The manager said that he knew that he could rely on everyone to make the change a success.

Kevin felt depressed. Then he began to feel angry about the changes and became resentful that 'they' should make these changes without understanding what it was that people really did.

It may well be that the only concern of which Kevin might be totally aware is whether or not he would in future have the time to fulfil his acting interests. However, the threat he senses is also to several other things that are part of his psychological contract: a job he knows he can do, the team he belongs to and liking to work for his supervisor. Even deeper down may be a real fear of computers and a half-hidden worry that he will be found wanting when he has to modernize his approach. The fact that not all these things are inevitable is not relevant to how he feels. In many ways, the uncertainty about how he, specifically, will be affected adds to his resistance to the change.

Other causes of resistance

❑ *Resentment at an imposed change*
   This may be a particularly potent cause when the person affected by the change feels very remote from the person instigating the change. This can occur when head office insists on a new approach to strategic planning that, if the change is not managed effectively, has the power to generate resistance in every manager affected by the edict. There may

be nothing wrong with the new approach, but this will not stop people who feel this kind of resentment from trying to block the new method and arguing that it does not fit their particular business. If you have never felt this form of resistance yourself, think of the furore that sometimes follows a new edict from the European Union Commissioners in Brussels. The reaction is often unrelated to the quality of the measure; it is because 'they' have done it.

❏ *Lack of trust in the leaders*
There are two types of lack of trust. The first is when the employees do not believe that the leader is telling them the truth, so therefore can accept neither the official vision of the benefits of the change nor any reassurances given to them by the leader. The second is when probity is not in doubt, but the leader is thought to be incompetent.

❏ *Belief that the change is wrong*
The difficulty with this cause of resistance is that, although genuinely felt, it is not always objective. In some situations, it may be a symptom of resistance caused by, say, a perceived threat that then leads to an examination of the change, often without all the evidence, and an unconsciously biased conclusion. Sometimes it is the result of an unbiased assessment that reaches a different conclusion to that of the change leader. And sometimes it is based on information that an individual has, but which the manager leading the change does not have. Well-founded resistance may be a warning bell that should be heeded. However, it has to be heard early enough for this to happen. If you are about to move towards a ski jump, you need information about something wrong at the bottom *before* you launch into space. Once airborne, it makes matters worse to be trying to stop at a time when all attention should be focused on the landing.

❏ *Personal animosity*
Feelings can be distorted by dislike of the change leader or some other cause of resentment. In the new manager situation given in Chapter 2, an example of this was provided by the person who felt that he should have been made manag-

er of the department instead of the person chosen. Sometimes resistance may be brought on by no more than the personal chemistry between people.

❏ *Serving their own ends*
If a group of employees feels that it has power, it may try to use that power to stop something happening that it feels is not to its advantage. This was the case in the newspaper company situation looked at earlier.

HOW TO REDUCE RESISTANCE TO CHANGE

Before looking at ways in which resistance might be reduced, it is worth thinking about Kevin, the accounting clerk in the example earlier in the chapter. In the change situation in which he finds himself, his resistance may not matter very much if he is the only person who feels it and, in this case, there is a good possibility that peer pressure will turn him around. He does not seem to be the sort of person who is a natural leader of opinion, who would spread the poison of his resentment. If there are many at his level who feel similarly, the position could be more serious. It may manifest itself in low motivation and poor morale, which can make people achieve less instead of the more they are expected to after the change.

There may be a belief that if the change does not work, the organization will revert to the old structure, leading to actions such as:

❏ following rules when the circumstances do not fit them and initiative should be used instead;
❏ failure to do anything outside the job description;
❏ not sharing any information that might affect the success of the change;
❏ time wasting;
❏ deliberate sabotage (Kevin would not do this, and neither would many other people, but it would need only one resentful person to sabotage the use of the new computers by introducing a virus into all of them).

When it is managers who are resistant, the potential to frustrate the change is even greater than it is with the rank and file. Instructions may be ignored, actions not completed and their departments given misleading information. The more senior the manager, the greater the risk that severe resistance will cause real problems.

Although, as we have seen, the urgency of the change will affect the amount of effort we can expend on trying to overcome resistance, there are usually some things that can be done. Understanding what these are will help you make the choices that are needed as you lead a change. This understanding also helps in making sense of the EASIER change model, which is the subject of the next chapter.

Anticipating resistance and removing causes

If the areas that will stimulate resistance are known, it is sometimes possible to take action to remove them. In the example of Kevin, the manager had identified one such cause – fear of redundancy – and gave an assurance that this would not happen. The two questions to consider are whether or not he could have been aware of the other causes of possible resistance and, if he had been so aware, could he have taken any action to overcome them? There were about 50 people in the department, so the manager should have known each of them moderately well, and his undermanagers and supervisors between them would know much more about each person. It may have been possible in this case for some reasonable assumptions to have been made about what would cause resistance and to anticipate these either by changing how the meeting was handled and the information disseminated or by pre-empting some of the causes. We do not know how long the manager had been planning this change, but, if there had been time, one way of removing the fear of computers might have been to give training in using them to Kevin and those like him in advance of the formal announcement.

I should like to defer to the next chapter any comment on how the change seems to have been handled, but you may care to think about this yourself now. Would your answers be the same if the department consisted of 150 people?

Participation

Participation has been shown to be very effective in reducing resistance, although, as we have already seen, there are different levels of participation and sometimes there is not enough time available to allow for this. It should also be accepted that participation is not a golden elixir and sometimes it will not make things better. In a few cases, it may be like giving an aspirin to someone who is dying from malaria, where it will not even have a placebo effect.

Some of the things participation may do are:

❑ create ownership of the proposed change as people feel that they have contributed to the decisions made;
❑ allow people to express their doubts and fears and receive answers to at least some of them;
❑ reduce frustration levels, by giving people a place to let off steam;
❑ ensure that everything about the change is both communicated and understood by those who will be affected;
❑ reduce the impact of rumour and gossip because people not only have the facts, but have been able to discuss them;
❑ bring more doubts and concerns into the open where they can be considered;
❑ reduce the level of uncertainty;
❑ change attitudes – getting people to work on the change in some way can often convince them that it is a good thing to do;
❑ make people may feel more in control, depending on the nature of the participation, which reduces stress levels.

Apart from the factors previously discussed, such as the requirement for extreme confidentiality and urgency, managers may be reluctant to involve others because:

❏ the sheer numbers of people make it very difficult (in which case, it may be desirable to achieve participation by working through the different levels of the structure and delegating parts of the task to others);

❏ an organization is not a democracy and so it is rarely possible to decide everything by popular vote (change has to be led and the nature of participation does not have to be the same for each level of the hierarchy, so it is possible to involve many more people in the 'how' of making a change work than in the determination of the change itself);

❏ there are weaknesses in the manager leading the change (some people do not like opening themselves to questioning, cannot tolerate any form of criticism, will not deal honestly with any bad news and do not really care about the people whose lives they are affecting).

Kevin's manager was not leading an exercise in participation, he was informing people. Participation implies two-way communication.

Some questions to think about in relation to your own change

❏ Is participation desirable in the circumstances?
❏ Does anything prevent participation?
❏ If so, can it be removed?
❏ Who should participate? Key people? Those who report directly to you? Everyone affected?
❏ What is the scope for participation for each of your chosen groups:

  – in the change decision itself?
  – in the decisions about how to implement the change?
  – empowerment to determine what has to be done to achieve the objectives of the change within a key manager's own area?
  – consultation about all or any aspects of the change?

❏ How should participation be achieved for each group –
by means of :
   – individual discussion?
   – meetings?
   – working parties?
❏ Should you delegate some aspects of participation to
others?

Do not overlook the value of one-to-one meetings as a means of
consulting people and obtaining feedback. These may be organized according to groupings within the structure of the organization, although when the numbers are small there may be benefits in having the change manager meet every affected person
individually. This clearly is not possible once the numbers total
over about 30 or, rather, it *is* possible but could take too long. In
any case, when numbers are large, the change manager may be
too remote from the people for them to speak openly, which is
another reason for delegating the task further down the line.

Several points should be borne in mind when contemplating
such meetings:

❏ people will only be totally open with a person they trust and,
ideally, also respect;
❏ all concerns expressed must be treated as important, even if
the change manager thinks they are trivial;
❏ answers must be given honestly, with no bluffing;
❏ all promises to find out about something that cannot be
answered in the meeting must be kept;
❏ do not try to sell an individual on the personal benefits of the
change if they are illusory;
❏ put people at their ease, and ask questions of them that cannot be answered with a simple 'yes' or 'no' or that signal the
answer you want to hear (it is better, for example, to say
something like 'You still look troubled, what is worrying
you?' than 'Now that I've explained things, have you any
more concerns?')

COMMUNICATION

Communication is important in all change situations, including those where participation is not desirable and a directive or coercive approach is used instead. The participative methods already discussed are, in part, a form of communication and have the merit of being two-way, in that those receiving the message can ask questions and make their own views and concerns known. Even when the change manager is using such methods, there is usually a need to reinforce this with other ways of communicating. The more complicated the situation and the greater the number of people affected by the change, the more need there is to develop a communications strategy to support the change.

The issue is so important that some organizations go to great lengths to supplement meetings with other forms of communication. Examples include a special publication explaining the change and the reasons for it, a special change newsletter that reports progress (obviously only useful for a change that is expected to take some time to implement fully, such as a new approach to customer care), internal videos, notices, internal e-mail and voice mail, personal letters to those affected, company newsletters and journals, and even interviews with outside journalists and broadcasters so that the change is widely reported. British Petroleum invited a *Financial Times* journalist to the board meetings where it was decided that its new focus and related culture change programme (project 1990) was necessary in order to ensure wide coverage of the change. It is worth considering a training initiative as a way of communicating the details of a change, gaining a measure of participation and equipping people with the skills they will need to be effective in their jobs after the change has been implemented.

If yours is a small change, relative to the organization as a whole, some of these choices may be closed to you, but do not use this as an excuse for confining your communications efforts to pinning a memo on the noticeboard. It needs something more than this.

How does effective communication help? Many of the answers to this question are obvious, but not so obvious that they are not often overlooked by organizations once they are in the turmoil of a change situation:

❏ it helps to reduce resistance by ensuring that the change is fully understood, as are the reasons for its having to be made;
❏ if done well, it helps people to realize that the organization has given some thought to them; if done badly, the opposite may occur;
❏ if there is a crisis, it ensures that everyone understands and this will reduce resistance as when there is a widespread awareness of a crisis, most people are less resistant to change and find directive approaches acceptable, even, sometimes, preferable;
❏ managing people's expectations is very important during a fundamental change situation, and this is impossible without good communications.

There are some things that should be considered, over and above the obvious decisions about media, when a communications strategy is developed:

❏ identify the target groups that should be communicated with and consider any differences in content and media that are required in order to reach these groups;
❏ determine what should be communicated;
❏ decide on the style of communication for each target group (and be careful not to be patronizing or treat people as simpletons);
❏ check whether or not the messages being communicated address the concerns that those affected by the change are likely to have;
❏ ensure that other communications from the organization do not undermine what you are trying to put across.

This last point requires a little elaboration, and a real example will help in this. Acrow is a company in the UK that went into liquidation during the 1980s. It had been a major organization that had built on its market leadership in scaffold poles, and, at the time of liquidation, its business embraced cranes, containers, excavators, agricultural equipment and other products. The company owned minority shares in other companies around the world, which were licensed by the UK firm to make and sell the Acrow brand of scaffold pole in particular countries.

In the few years before its failure, the company was going through a very difficult time, resulting in factory closures and consolidations, job losses and great concern over its ability to survive. Yet, the message in every issue of the company journal was that the business was a success. What was not made clear in all the reports of major Acrow contracts around the world was that most had little impact on the company's results (the only impact was via the dividends it received from its minority investments) and no impact at all on the utilization of the capacity of its own factories. While it is possible to appreciate that the journal was optimistic because it also went to customers, its tone regarding growth and expansion did not fit the crisis situation in which it was operating.

MANAGING THE SURVIVORS OF CHANGE

It is very easy to assume that in a change where there are redundancies, those people who keep their jobs will have feelings of relief and gratitude and work for the success of the organization with renewed vigour. This is one of the management myths of our time.

Survivors' reactions are affected by a number of variables, which include:

❏ The extent to which the redundancies were expected, in which case reactions may be more favourable than if the change was a bolt from the blue.
❏ The way in which the redundancies were announced. Even when the reasons for the redundancy are understood, nega-

tive feelings may be generated by the way in which the announcement was handled.

❑ How fair the selection procedures appeared to the survivors. Reactions are likely to be more adverse if the procedure seems to have been unfair.

❑ The degree to which the jobs of survivors and leavers are interdependent. The closer they are, the more the survivors will identify with those who have to leave.

❑ How closely those leaving resemble those staying in skills and attitudes. We identify more with people like ourselves than those we see as being very different.

❑ How insecure the survivors feel, which is related to the chances that those who leave have of finding other jobs and the personal experiences of previous redundancies of those who remain with the organization. The higher the level of insecurity, the greater will be the adverse reactions of the survivors.

❑ The level of attention given to helping the survivors to cope with the new situation. Where the redundancies mean that the survivors have to work in a different way or apply different skills and competencies, reactions will be more severe if the survivors feel that they have been thrown in at the deep end and expected to find their own way out, whether or not they can swim.

The attitudes and feelings of survivors manifest themselves in their behaviour. Typically, survivors may experience:

❑ guilt that they have not lost their jobs when other equally good people have had to go;

❑ disbelief and a sense of betrayal ('They would not do this to us', followed by 'How could they do this to us?');

❑ anger and animosity;

❑ lack of commitment, low morale and feelings of insecurity.

These can convert into absenteeism, lack of initiative, resignations of people the organization needs to keep and poorer performance. In turn, such attitudes can lead to increased stress and genuine illness among at least some of the survivors. It is all very much like resistance to change except that the survivors are not resisting, they are reacting to the change. They have no hope of turning the clock back to prevent the change.

It is not possible to remove every negative feeling, but effective management of the redundancy situation can reduce many of them. A glance at the variables shows several places where the manager is in control:

❏ The expectations of survivors can be managed, by showing that there is an awareness of the underlying problem. This is most easily achieved when the organization has an established briefing process, so that good and bad news affecting the employees are shared on a regular basis.
❏ A vision of what the changes will mean for the future should be provided so that some of the uncertainty of survivors is removed.
❏ Announcements can be made in a manner that does not shock or leave the impression that the organization does not care about those sacked.
❏ Redundancies can be handled in a way that is not only fair, but is *seen* to be fair.
❏ Employees can be given coaching and training to help them ease into their new roles.
❏ Advice and help can sometimes be given to those made redundant to support them in their search for new jobs.

The next chapter will explore the next two steps in our approach to change management: the EASIER model, which, if followed, will avoid many of the typical problems of a change situation, and defining the point when we can decide that the change has been fully implemented.

5

WORKING THROUGH THE CHANGE PROCESS

In the previous chapter we looked at Kevin's situation and the meeting at which the manager of his department announced a number of changes. Regardless of whether or not the appropriate style was chosen by the manager to announce this change, it is possible to see how the conduct of this meeting contributed to Kevin's feelings of resistance. No good reason was given to explain the need for change, and this would only be excusable if previous briefings and communications had ensured that everyone already knew that a cost reduction was imperative and why. No vision of what the department would achieve or be like after the change was provided, and the mention of additional computers seemed to be more of a random event than part of a thought out manifestation of how the department would be different. At the stage the manager seemed to have reached, the new structure should have been known and many concerns could have been removed by either giving the details at the meeting or having smaller meetings with those concerned immediately afterwards, so that the details could be explained. Kevin might have found that he was still in the same work group, for example. The way the meeting was conducted gave no opportunity for two-way communication, and even a directive approach should have allowed people to seek clarification by asking questions. There is much more about the meeting that could be criticized, but we will have to leave Kevin to his problems.

The EASIER approach offers a six-step change management process that, if followed, will help the change to be managed more effectively. After the approach has been described, we will test it in the next chapter by applying it to the new manager situation mentioned in Chapter 1. This situation has been chosen because it is typical of many changes that a manager will handle during a normal career. If you want to work through a complicated fundamental change situation, you might like to spend a few minutes thinking how you would apply the model if you were managing the change in the lift company. Some clues have been provided in previous chapters, and occasional mention will be made of the lift company as the model is described.

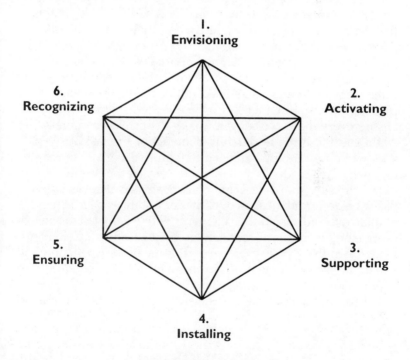

Figure 5.1 *The easier approach to managing change*

Figure 5.1 shows the six steps of the model, called EASIER after the initial letters of each label on the figure. The mnemonic aids the memory, but the connecting lines in the diagram are important because none of the steps can be said to be complete until the whole change is implemented. This is partly because with a complicated change there may be some elements of phasing. We saw, for example, how Bill in the lift company wanted to ensure that his management team was committed to his vision before trying to share it with the rest of the organization. It is also because a successful change manager has to eat, sleep and breathe the change. Building commitment to the vision, for example, is an ongoing process that does not stop because the first elements of the change have reached a point when they can be monitored. Almost every action of the manager throughout the whole process should communicate the importance of the change.

The EASIER model contains two types of actions. The first three steps are the motivational and leadership elements of the process, which aim to inspire people, reduce resistance and ensure everyone is working to make the change a success. We could call these the leadership elements of the task. However, they will rarely succeed unless attention is also given to the second half of the model, which might be termed the administration of the change – the system and analytical tasks that clarify what has to be done and measure whether or not it has been achieved. Similarly, the administrative elements will usually fail to achieve change unless they are accompanied by the leadership elements. Even when the style is coercive – as in the newspaper company situation – some element of visionary leadership is required to inspire those who are not resistant to the change.

Let us now look at each of the steps in the EASIER model in turn.

1. ENVISIONING

There is widespread agreement that change management is more effective when the leader demonstrates a clear vision of the desired future. This need for a vision is not restricted to organizations. Many will remember Tony Blair in the run up to the 1997 general election talking frequently about his vision for the UK, as well as his vision for New Labour. A vision is much more than a statement of the change. 'We are going to downsize by 20 per cent' may be an accurate description of the change, but it is not a vision. What is needed is a view of what the organization will be as a result of the action and clarity about why the change is necessary to take the organization towards achieving that vision.

A vision is important for a number of reasons:

❑ it forces the change manager to think carefully not only about the course that is being set, but also about the destination and the time it will take to reach it;

❑ by defining the vision, further actions may be revealed that support the change, but might otherwise have been overlooked;

❑ the vision becomes a beacon that can be followed even though crises and other events requiring decisions occur on the way;

❑ it can help shape the expectations of the people affected by the change;

❑ it explains why the change is important;

❑ a sound and clear vision has the power to motivate others.

It is easy to see why vision is important for the large, complicated changes that affect the whole organization. However, it is just as important for the smaller changes, and both the toiletries company and the innovation situations described in Chapter 1 depend heavily on a clear vision if they are to succeed. Even for changes that affect only a unit of an organization, the change is likely to be more effective if the leader is clear about the desired destination.

A vision must be:

❑ *credible* – it must relate to the situation the organization is in and the resources it can command;

❑ *challenging* – it must paint a picture that people will want to

strive to achieve;
- ❏ *clear* – if it cannot be plainly set out, it is unlikely to be understood;
- ❏ *logical* – all the elements of the vision must fit together;
- ❏ have the *total commitment* of the manager leading the change – if this appears to be absent, there is no reason for anyone else to believe in it;
- ❏ *robust* – it has to be able to withstand challenges from within and without the organization.

2. ACTIVATING

The next step shown in Figure 5.1 is the process of making sure that those affected by the change are aware of the vision, understand it and, ideally, share the vision and are committed to its fulfilment. As we have seen, there may be circumstances when we have to settle for knowledge and understanding as urgency or the strength of resistance make it almost impossible to proceed with anything other than a directive or coercive style. It is true that in a crisis everyone recognizes as being urgent, it may be possible to reach a shared vision by directive means. Normally, a shared vision will only be achieved in the short term by means of a more participative style, although it is sometimes sensible to vary the style to meet the situations of different groups or levels of those affected by the change.

If it is hard to define a vision, it is even harder to activate others so that they share the commitment to it. When the situation allows, a shared vision can be very powerful in making the change more effective:

- ❏ it provides a focus so that everyone pulls in the same direction, which makes it easier to empower people in a way that aids the change process;
- ❏ resistance is minimized by means of the process of involvement;
- ❏ the adverse consequences of change may be more readily

accepted because the expectations of people are shaped by the acceptance of the common cause;

❏ after the change, people are more likely to integrate the vision into their day-to-day work and, therefore, continue acting in a way that supports the vision;

❏ a well-accepted vision can become a powerful motivational force in the organization.

One of the tasks of the change leader is thus to build a bridge from the vision that they have defined to others affected by the change. Obviously the task is simpler when the change occurs in a small unit of four or five people than when it applies to the whole of a major multinational organization, but the principles by which it may be achieved are the same:

❏ The change manager must live the vision and be seen to be a perpetual demonstration of what it is and what it means. Actions – the music – speak louder than words – the song – and it becomes clear very quickly when the lyrics have little to do with the tune.

❏ Words are important and one-to-one, often informal, ways should be found of repeating the message, checking how people are responding and demonstrating its importance.

❏ There is a place for the explanatory meetings that describe the vision and all the supporting documentation, but these should be seen as only a small element of the process.

❏ Ensure that those who report to you are charged with the duty of building commitment to the vision among those who report to them.

❏ Continuously seek out and disseminate evidence of success. Most changes are achieved by means of numerous small actions as well as a few large ones. Evidence of the results of the sort of behaviour and actions that you want to see should be occurring all the time, and can be used to show what the vision means.

❏ Make sure that the vision is made relevant at the level of each job. In a large organization, this is too large a task to do single-handed and is another reason for getting some key people involved in the process very early on. However, this should not stop the change manager from continuing to talk to people about the vision at all levels of the organization.

❏ Learn from the things that do not appear to be going as well as expected. If the problem is caused by pockets of resistance, take special steps to try to reduce them. In extreme situations this may mean sidelining or even dismissing someone who is using guerilla warfare tactics to frustrate the change.

❏ Use routine management meetings to emphasize the message.

❏ Where it is possible, set up a series of workshops to enable a wide range of people to help determine how the vision will affect their departments and jobs.

❏ Ensure that there is a communications strategy (see Chapter 4).

❏ Exude absolute confidence about the change and the future that it will lead to.

❏ Be sure that the vision is reinforced by the systems and procedures of the organization (see Chapter 3).

3. SUPPORTING

Change may put great pressures on people. One of the change manager's key tasks is to help subordinates to cope. Much of the support may be psychological, giving encouragement and empathizing, but sometimes it is necessary to give more practical help, by rearranging responsibilities or adding new resources, for example. The change manager has to ensure that the people have the necessary skills and competencies to undertake the new roles and activities that are required by the change.

As we have seen, people may resist change because they fear that they lack the abilities to take on the different challenge. Even supportive people may find that the change is making them less effective if it is causing them to neglect other aspects of their work that have not changed, say, or increases stress to danger levels or because they simply lack the knowledge and experience to do what is expected of them. The support step in the EASIER model is thus critical for success and, because it is bound up with the activating step, may also aid the process of building commitment to the vision.

Actions that should be taken by the change manager include:

❑ Making sure that the way you have allocated tasks is with an awareness of the individual strengths and weaknesses of your subordinates, and that thereafter you regularly demonstrate your confidence in them to deliver what is expected.

❑ Where it is needed, providing training at an early stage to provide missing skills and build confidence.

❑ Making coaching a regular part of your activity, so that you are not only listening to what you are being told, but are actively helping people by giving them suggestions, advice and encouragement. Make coaching a positive experience.

❑ Never treating their concerns as trivial, but always be empathizing with their problems and trying to help them find ways of overcoming them.

❑ Empowering people to fulfil the tasks you have asked them to do. Part of the challenge the change manager faces is that of leaving a feeling of total confidence in the person, while at the same time having regular contact to give the necessary support. This tightrope is not easy to walk as badly handled discussions can be construed as an attempt to control, and inept coaching may be seen as preventing the person from being empowered.

❑ When there are real problems, such as inadequate resources to implement the change, offering real solutions. The skill here is to separate the roadblocks erected by those resisting change from the genuine issues of those who are trying to do the right things.

❑ Praising people when it is justified. If someone has done something that should be shared among others working on the change, either get that person to pass on details of it to the others or ask if you may do so.

4. INSTALLING

Installing is perhaps not the best description of the next step in the model, but none of the better words begin with an 'I'! It is the first element of the system and analysis part of the EASIER model, and is critical to success. In essence, it is the development of a thoughtful plan for the change. A broad vision of the change is important for all the reasons discussed so far and provides a context for the change, but little will happen unless the vision is converted into strategies, and the strategies into actions. In this context, the term 'strategies' is used very broadly to cover the means by which the vision is attained. It may have its normal meaning when the change is complicated and corporate-wide, and the change is about reshaping the whole organization to meet the challenge of the future. However, it is also an appropriate word to use to describe the means by which even the simplest of changes is converted from an idea into action. It covers questions such as what are the main strands that have to be followed and, under each of these, what are the actions that have to be undertaken? This is a way of thinking that is appropriate in every change situation and, of course, would include not only the many physical things, such as the new layout of the factory in the lift company situation, but also the many things we have already discussed that facilitate the change process, such as the communications strategy.

The process that has been followed so far will have provided you with many of the building blocks you need to make a detailed plan – from an assessment of the implications of the change, which was described in Chapter 2, to defining the vision and describing the change and the reasons for it, which were discussed under the heading of envisioning earlier in this chapter.

The installation step can be undertaken by the change manager alone, with the support of one or two specialists, or as part of a more participative process. If you have adopted a directive style, the choice is almost certain to be restricted to the first two. For a more participative style, it is often desirable to involve more people in the planning process, although the nature of the involvement may vary with different groups or at different levels of the organization. For example, in the lift company situation, we saw that Bill was involving his senior managers in thinking through everything that needed to be done to implement the change, and was doing this initially in a workshop-style meeting. In another situation, or possibly even at a later stage in the lift company's change process, it might be desirable to have someone visit all those people at any level who can contribute insights into what the change would mean, to identify all the steps in much greater detail. Where the change involves only a few people and is contained within the responsibility of a unit or department, it may be that the manager already possesses all the knowledge needed to prepare a detailed plan without involving anyone. Whether the plan is put together in this way or by means of a process that involves more people depends on the style chosen for the change management, and if the plan offers an opportunity to involve others if it is sensible in the circumstances.

There is a caution that we need to make known here about who to involve in preparing a detailed plan. If the unit is very small, it is possible to include everyone, if this is appropriate. In most change situations, however, it is not desirable to involve everyone in the same way. For example, in the lift company situation, it would frustrate the change if, immediately after the management meeting that examined the implications of the change, the whole factory was called together and everyone asked to work on the detail before the changes had been agreed with the worker's representatives: it is simply an inappropriate type of change to throw out to the shop floor like this. However, a more local change could well involve people in this way. For example, a problem of high material wastage might be discussed with the people who use the material and, ultimately, a plan to correct it worked out with their participation.

Whatever the choice of process, the aims of this step in the change model are the same:

❑ as far as is humanly possible, to think through everything that has to be done to implement the change;

❏ to assign responsibilities so that those who have to take actions know what is expected;
❏ clarify all the detailed goals of the plan so they can be communicated to all concerned;
❏ provide a basis for monitoring progress;
❏ ensure that the necessary resources of people, facilities and money are determined and made available so that the plan can be implemented.

This last point deserves further comment. A change can be frustrated if resources are neglected, and the time to provide for those resources is *before* the organization commits itself to the change. An example is offered by the lift company case, where there is a need for some building work and costs will be incurred in changing the layout of the shop floor. The resources for this have to be agreed up front for without them it will not be possible to make the change. A more subtle example is the need to train managers and those they manage in the new methods of working that need to be adopted after a downsizing operation.

Part of the change management task is to see that the right training is provided, and quickly, and this will not happen unless the right provisions are made. Downsizing may prove to be futile without the training, so it is essential that it happen. To be told by the human resources department that the budget for the year is already committed or that this is not a priority or that training can only be given over a two-year period is to set the change on the path to failure.

Not all changes require the same planning tools and some thought should be given to selecting what is appropriate to a particular situation:

❏ *Simple action plans*
Where the situation is straightforward, involves only a few people and requires no additional resources, it may be enough for a plan to take the form of a simple listing of the actions that have to be undertaken, dates for start and completion and the name of the person responsible. This should be written down, but is not difficult.

❏ *Short-term plan and project budget*
This is a combined action plan and worked budget. This should list all the actions to be taken (in much the same way as the simple plan), provide time commitments and short-term goals so that progress can be monitored and provide a budget that shows both the expenses and the financial consequences of the change. The project budget may well cut across the normal responsibility centres, so it is advisable to ensure that the accounting system can report against this budget, which is likely to fall outside the normal budgetary process. Some special provision may need to be made so that regular reporting is possible. The timespan of the budget has to be capable of being divided into normal accounting periods, but should encompass the whole of the change project. It may span more than one accounting year, and may be for longer than the 12-month period of the normal budget.

A refinement of the short-term plan would be to also show the actions and responsibilities on a Gantt chart, which lists all the actions against a calendar and shows by means of lines when each will start and finish. This is helpful in that it is easier to discuss with others than a long action list, and it does begin to indicate where a delay in one action may cause delays in others.

❏ *Network analysis*
Some change projects may involve thousands of actions and change may be frustrated if critical tasks are delayed, while others can be allowed to drift within a wider tolerance as this will not delay the whole project. In a change such as that in the lift company, it would be difficult to estimate how long the whole change would take just by listing the actions, as some can be tackled simultaneously while others have to be done in strict sequence. What is needed is a tool that not only pulls all this information together in a way that can easily be communicated, but also enables those planning the change to see where things might be done quicker if more or different resources were used. Carrying out one of the simultane-

ous actions earlier than planned would probably have no impact on the overall length of time it would take to complete the change project. However, allocating extra resources to one of the critical actions could reduce the overall time period for the whole project. Network analysis tools, such as critical path analysis, can be used in simple situations, although this may be taking a sledgehammer to crack a nut. They become essential, however, for the complicated projects, where actions can otherwise be easily overlooked or critical actions allowed to run late simply because there are so many things to do. Used in conjunction with a project budget, they enable every action to be closely monitored.

❑ *Scenario planning, sensitivity analysis and contingency planning*
The really large projects can benefit from an analysis that helps the manager to react more flexibly in the event of unexpected obstacles. They are of limited value in all but the largest of change projects.

Scenario planning is the development of alternative project plans based on different scenarios of the future. It is especially helpful when there are serious uncertainties about the likely outcomes of the change. It enables the organization to take action more quickly when events are not working out exactly as intended.

Sensitivity analysis is a means of looking at what issues could cause the project to go wrong, and what the impact might be. Whereas scenario plans, in effect, look at whole different futures that could occur, sensitivity analysis examines only the impact of particular issues.

Contingency plans are fully worked out alternative plans to be put into effect if something goes wrong. In the lift company situation, there might be a contingency plan for how to proceed with the change if the shop stewards recommend rejection to their members.

5. ENSURING

If a change takes only days to fully implement, and it can be seen very easily that it has worked, the 'ensuring' step is not needed. There are changes like that, but they are probably not the sorts of changes that will tax management skills. Most changes, however, take some time to be implemented, require constant coordination and depend on things being done at the appropriate time. There may also be expenditures of either a capital or revenue nature that have to be managed.

The ensuring step in the EASIER model is about monitoring and controlling progress. There really is little point in making a detailed plan unless there is also a mechanism to measure its progress. Monitoring is the process of collecting information that shows what progress has been made, while controlling is the management task of taking whatever actions are needed when the results deviate from the plan, and congratulating people when a difficult stage has been successfully completed. The following points should be borne in mind regarding these means of measuring progress:

❑ Monitoring requires a system for the collection and feedback of information on actual results compared to those planned. It may be necessary to make special arrangements to obtain this information where it does not emerge as part of normal accounting system reporting.

❑ In any case, some data will be required that does not come out of normal systems, such as the actual progress of actions against what was planned, information from special surveys or customer reactions to a new approach. Some means have to be devised to capture such information on a regular and formal basis.

❑ There should be regular feedback reports, some of which, such as those for time-critical things, may be more frequent than others. Thus, it may be appropriate to have a report of expenditure against budget at monthly intervals, but critical to know immediately whether or not a key action has been started or completed on the dates set.

❑ Modern communication methods, such as e-mail and voice mail, should be considered as a means of collecting information.
❑ Regular performance meetings should be held so that key members of the management team can assess progress, and take such actions as are necessary. These meetings should also be used to collect 'soft' information that does not fit easily into more formal reports and reinforce the vision and the importance of the change.
❑ The style of the control meetings should fit with the style for the whole change project. It would be wrong to have a collaborative style up to and including the installation step, for example, only to switch to a coercive style in the control meetings.
❑ The best control is self-control, which is when you have reached a stage when every manager knows their role is critical and is always self-monitoring against the appropriate part of the plan.

6. RECOGNIZING

The final step in the model is recognizing the parts played by others in the change process. It is very rare that a complicated change is accomplished without others besides the change manager playing an important part.

Recognition may be connected with career development and monetary incentives, but this is only one aspect. It may, in fact, be more productive to use recognition as a way of acknowledging what others have done and expressing thanks for this. The simple process of demonstrating that their role has been valued can mean a great deal, when the recipients see it as a sincere gesture.

There may be a place for team recognition. One multinational food group, for example, has an annual chairman's award for the initiative that has had most impact on the company. One year this was given to the team that had initiated and introduced across the whole organization an approach that enabled management development to be a weapon of competitive advantage.

The effect on the team was to increase its already high level of motivation because its efforts had been acknowledged to the whole organization. Obviously if the annual award had been seen as a joke, the impact would have been negative. In this case, however, it was highly prized.

Although it is the last step in the EASIER model, recognizing people's contributions does not have to wait until the change has been completed. It may, in fact, be part of the ongoing process. There are several things to consider:

❑ Make the change part of the performance management process. Also, where the change extends over a long period, ensure that you have several review meetings with your subordinates and that they repeat this process for key people who report to them. This not only helps to reinforce the vision and the importance of the change, but gives the manager a chance to recognize what the others have contributed or take action when performance in relation to implementing the change has been less than satisfactory.

❑ Recognition has to be genuine, which means that praise should only be given when it is due and should be sincerely expressed. Thanking someone for their help when both parties know that more effort has gone into frustrating the change than to making it effective, would turn the process into a travesty. Equally unproductive is a murmur of thanks that is no more than a social pleasantry as this will be taken to have little meaning and may leave the person concerned feeling that the change manager is ignorant of the important role they have really fulfilled.

❑ It is usually better to be very specific in one-to-one meetings. 'Thank you for your support' is a bland statement that has much less meaning to the receiver than 'It was the way you got down to it and came back quickly with those stories of how positive the customers were that got all the doubters on board. We never looked back from that moment'. The latter does not have the word 'thanks' in it, but shows that the change manager knows what the contribution was and is making a sincere acknowledgement of it.

❏ Public acknowledgement may sometimes be a powerful tool, but can cause embarrassment if it is not handled carefully, and it can come across as insincere (even when it is sincere). Think for a moment of some of those acceptance speeches made by film stars when they have been given an Oscar. So many seem to rattle off acknowledgements to every other person concerned in the film – 'I could not have done it without ...' – when everyone listening knows that what they really mean is 'I've got to say all this, but really it was all down to me and at last I have the award that I have long deserved'.

❏ Often more important than public recognition is making the part played by someone who has been important in making the change work known to the change manager's boss. It is probably best to say this to the boss in the presence of the person acknowledged. If the acknowledgement is of a team, then it may be better to ask the boss to come to meet them, and make the comments there. In both cases, giving specific examples of what others have done may be more meaningful than making a generalized statement. There is real value in the change manager making it clear to the team that credit for the change is being shared. Unfortunately, the change manager can rarely spread responsibility for a failure in the same way, which is another very good reason for making every effort to ensure that the change is effective.

KNOWING WHEN TO CALL A HALT TO THE CHANGE PROCESS

All things come to an end and there will come a time when the change can be safely declared to have been implemented. With some change projects this point is not difficult to identify. For others, however, it may be very difficult to decide where the halting place should be. In the lift company example, is the change completed when people have agreed to it, the factory has been laid out according to the new requirements, all the capital needed for the change has been spent and any initial training has been completed? This would be the stopping place for many change managers, but it is too early. The change can only be declared to have been effective when the new ways of managing have bedded down, employees have developed a strong affinity with their focused groups and the product quality, cost and delivery objectives have been achieved. The threat of closure is not removed until the factory is delivering products that can sustain their competitiveness relative to the competing plants in the group.

Determining the cut-off point requires an ability to think beyond the immediate future and develop an understanding of all the implications of the change (see Chapter 3). Failure to do this may help explain the persistent failure rates for acquisitions, where inadequate attention is given to what happens after the shares have been acquired and top management switches attention after signing the deal. This does not explain all acquisition failure, but accounts for a great deal of it. The change has to be managed to the point where the acquisition is integrated and able to deliver the vision that lay behind the purchase.

Once the right cut-off point has been determined, the change manager's final task is to ensure a smooth transition from the change situation to normal management. Often this means reshaping processes such as performance management, changing the selection criteria for promotion or recruitment and ensuring that the key managers continue to sustain the vision behind the change. Once again, for many changes, it is a question of thinking beyond the immediate future.

The sad thing is that a successful change can be thrown into reverse almost by accident unless management continues to sustain it.

6

APPLYING THE CHANGE PROCESS

In Chapter 2, we left Anne, the new manager of the information department, with the task of implementing a change. She had only a small department, but faced a mix of high and low resistance. The recommendation we made in Chapter 2 was for her to try a participative approach, but be prepared to take a more directive tone with any managers when their resistance could not be overcome. Before we examine how Anne might use the EASIER approach, we should look at some more information to gain a better understanding of the nature of the change.

Situation 5, part 2: the new manager

The information department had evolved from the company library, although it now relied heavily on computer-based sources of information. Its main paper-based sources were a large collection of directories and some long runs of relevant journals. It subscribed to some press cutting services and kept some files of cuttings of its own on a number of subjects.

At her interviews, Anne had been told little about the causes of dissatisfaction with the department, beyond the statement that it had the potential to add great value to the organization, but was not currently doing so.

Anne soon reached the conclusion that the department was rather passive. It responded to requests for information (usually by dialling one of the database services it subscribed to or calling up the sources on the Internet), and passed what it found back to the person who had requested it. The purpose for which the information was requested was rarely known. Occasionally a manager would explain what the information was for and ask for a report instead of raw information, but this was unusual. The most-praised reports of this nature, although few in number, had been prepared by John – the person who resented her appointment.

Among the many other tasks of the department was the sorting of press cuttings into weekly packs by subject and then passing these out to various people in the organization. Some packs were about 50 pages long, often with the same story written up by different newspapers, and some managers received several subject packs. The department also scrutinized the journals it took and added its own clippings from these sources. There were other activities, too, such as obtaining books or journals, and the coordination of information from various abstract services.

Anne reported to a director of administration, who in turn reported to the managing director. Her department was a very small part of the director's overall responsibility.

In her first few days in the company, Anne was very careful not to appear critical of the way the department had operated. She told her team that she needed to understand the company and felt that her role was to ensure that the department added value to the organization. She asked all her team, including the secretary, to let her have ideas on how value might be added and she herself visited all the other areas of the company to assess what they really wanted from the department. There was pressure from her director for immediate action.

Anne pulled together all the information she had obtained from her survey and her team and her conclusions included a number of major changes. First, she wanted the department to be more active and to sift and analyse information before passing it on. This would mean that her team would have to discuss the purpose of the information with the person wanting it and integrate what was obtained from external sources with information from the internal management system (which was also available on-line and, if her staff were researching a customer, for example, their report could also include information on sales to the customer by the whole organization and the department requesting the information). The report would draw conclusions. Another manifestation of the new approach was that the press cuttings would be handled differently. Instead of large packages of paper going to everyone, there would be a weekly analysis of what had appeared, with only one or two cuttings attached, and a directory of other cuttings that could be supplied on request. The department would make more sense of the subject files, making periodic analyses of key areas and ensuring that managers were alerted to anything of importance.

In order to free up time for the new tasks, Anne intended to give other managers direct access to the database services so that they could look up basic information themselves. Sometimes all that was wanted was the latest published results of a competitor or customer and the person who wanted this information could access the database in the same time it normally took to contact the information department and put in a request.

Now Anne had to make the new ideas work.

Note that in Table 2.1 in Chapter 2, it was suggested that the change affected Anne's department only. This is not totally true. However, there is no compulsion for other departments to change how they work and evidence to suggest that she is responding to their desire for change. The assessment made in the table was such because she does not face a major task in managing change outside the areas of her own responsibility.

HOW THE EASIER APPROACH COULD BE APPLIED

Before reading further, you might care to spend a few minutes making a few notes on how you would manage the change if you were Anne. One point to remember is that, although the change is internal to her department, it will have an effect on the 'customers' – the various managers who use the service – who seem to want the changes. She can still provide the former service to anyone who wants to continue as before, but will not achieve much if this happens.

1. Envisioning

From what we know so far, we can assume that Anne has made a thorough investigation and has thought through the implications of the change she proposes. This does not mean that there is nothing she has missed, but she has got a good handle on what the change will mean.

Her next task should be to formulate her vision of the department, to at least draft stage. Components of that vision might include:

❑ an intention to be a department that is adding value in the company, supporting managers at both strategic and operational levels;

❑ priorities of the department being based on the priorities of the company;

❑ the department playing a consulting role by merging information from different sources, analysing the implications and delivering usable reports to managers;

❑ the department becoming critical to the future success of the company.

Anne will need to refine these headings, but, given her intention to use a participative style, she might well involve her department in this as part of the next step, activating. However, she must be able to conceptualize her vision before this happens and have total belief that this is the way forward. The vision will become important beyond her department when she takes action to try to ensure that all the users of the information department work with her on the value adding approach.

Another decision she needs to make is whether or not to withhold the draft from the rest of the organization until it is finalized or to discuss it in outline, along with the changes that will follow, with some of the key managers who will use the service and her own boss. My inclination would be to share it on a selective basis – if only to make sure that she has captured the needs of the users – but to keep these discussions informal and confidential until all the details have been worked out.

Other stages of the envisioning process include deciding how to explain the urgency and underlying need for the change, which she has not yet done except in the most general way, and setting out the proposed changes in reasonable detail.

2. Activating

Rather than polish the vision statement and produce a final version herself, it would make sense for Anne to ask her team to help her.

In presenting the draft vision to her team, she would have the advantage of the objective findings of her research and should share the pressures that she is under to make the department fit better with the requirements of the organization. She should avoid any temptation to criticize how the department was run in the past and, instead, should emphasize what is needed now and for the future as a new situation.

As in the lift company situation, there is a need to think through the implications of the changes she wants to make. Although she has done this fairly thoroughly herself, she has the opportunity to begin the activating phase by working with her small team to refine the vision, assess all the implications and ensure that the changes she proposes are understood and discussed.

A meeting of her department is probably the best way to do this, although she would no doubt have some trepidation about this with regard to the two people she sees as trying to resist any change. She has already given the department a small involvement in the assessment work leading up to the proposed change (it would have been possible to make this more collaborative than she did if she had not had severe doubts about some team members).

At the meeting, Anne must lead, but this does not mean that she should be inflexible and unwilling to fine-tune the vision or the actions based on the input of her team. She might also take the opportunity to find further ways to bring the resistors on board. For example, John's reports are evidence of the sort of change the organization wants. If she uses this as an example of success, it may make it harder for John to argue against at least this part of the change, and if others are less experienced, she could also ask John to run an internal workshop to train them in this type of report writing. Another approach might be to divide the task of telling all other managers about the change between the members of the team. If she has already cleared the draft vision with senior managers, the task of dealing with the other users could be delegated in this way. By working on making the change work, there is a good chance that the doubters will convince themselves of the vision.

Anne must continue to work on sharing the vision *after* the meeting at every opportunity. Major successes should be shared with everyone.

3. Supporting

The main support that Anne will need to give during this change is likely to be the coaching of each person on a fairly regular basis, to help them all operate in the new way. Any additional specific training should also be provided, and she should be willing to listen to any concerns people might have. She may also have to be willing to speak to users where there appears to be a difficulty between them and her staff, to try to resolve any problems.

4. Installing

It is unlikely that her implementation plan will be very complicated, so a simple action plan approach will be adequate. The important thing is to identify all tasks, determine when they should be done and who is to do them. Delegating as much as possible to her team will continue to involve them in the change.

The sorts of actions that might be planned could include training for users who want to access the databases directly, designing the new analysis reports of the press cuttings, implementing this change and collecting feedback from the users, setting up a programme for making sense of the filed material and developing some checklists for her team to use when asked to do something by the users. It would also make sense to plan some follow-up meetings with users after the first few reports have been delivered, to check that the content and style meets their needs.

5. Ensuring

In a small unit, Anne will see her team informally every day and so should have a fairly good idea how things are going. Formally, she should have a team meeting at least once a month or possibly more frequently if a lot of completion dates fall due earlier. This meeting can be used as a way of reinforcing the vision, sharing success stories and fine-tuning the actions. Sometimes Anne might want to invite one or two users to part of these meetings to share perceptions on their real needs and responses to the new approach.

6. Recognizing

When the change is in place and working, she might persuade the managing director to meet with her team, so that her people can see that the new approach is valued. At that point, she can make sure that the team knows that she is sharing the credit with them. The assumption so far is that John and the other resistor can be brought on board, but she also has to be prepared to take action if they do anything to frustrate the change.

Of course, there would be many more actions than have been suggested above and the whole change process would become more complicated if the organization had to be persuaded of its value, but enough has been said to show how the EASIER process might work in a situation like Anne's. It should also be stressed that things do not all happen sequentially and, thus, the model is not meant to be used as a checklist, the items being ticked off and forgotten once each step has been progressed. Almost every step will take place simultaneously with other steps and things will not all happen in a strict order.

WHAT DOES IT TAKE TO BE AN EFFECTIVE CHANGE MANAGER?

Table 6.1 is presented with some trepidation and many cautions. It makes the point that different stages in the change process require different things from the change manager. The table is rather general and will change with specific circumstances. For example, the knowledge section makes this very clear, and a quick glance back at the various situations given in Chapter 2 will show that the underlying knowledge needed is not identical in each situation.

There is also a danger that a list such as this looks more like a search for a candidate for canonization than for a normal human being. What we are really interested in is not so much the skills, knowledge and attributes, but the way the managers apply them in the change situation. It is management's behaviour that is important, and this may relate to only a part of what could be defined as a skill. However, the translation of skill to behaviour is also situational and would not be exactly the same in each of the change situations we have examined. It is also worth emphasizing that words such as 'integrity' refer to behaviour *during* the change process. In this context, it is possible for a manager who has been swindling the petty cash for years to act with integrity to those involved in the change process. So, the intention is not to pass judgement on the whole person, but to think of what lies behind some of the behaviours needed to make the process effective.

We also have some umbrella headings. For example, there are many subdivisions of something like 'communication skills'. A manager may be excellent at verbal communication and useless at producing a coherent, written statement of the vision.

The first purpose of Table 6.1 is not to say 'here is what you will need', but to offer a starting point from which you may begin to assess what you should be good at in order to apply the change approach set out in this book to your own situation. You may well need to add things to your list that do not appear in the table.

However, there is another purpose, which is to think about what a manager might do when the realization is reached that something that is needed is missing. The personal portfolio of capabilities might match well to all the steps except those of activating and support. Does this mean that the manager will be unable to be an effective change manager?

Table 6.1 *Skills, Knowledge and attributes required for change management*

What is needed	Implication	Stages in the change management process where attribute needed						
		1. Envisioning	*2.* Activating	*3.* Supporting	*4.* Installing	*5.* Ensuring	*6.* Recognizing	*7.* Right end
Skills								
Analytical	✗							
Coaching					✗	✗		✗
Communication	✗	✗	✗	✗				
Conceptualization	✗	✗	✗	✗			✗	✗
Counselling		✗	✗	✗	✗	✗		
Empowering			✗					
Listening	✗		✗	✗		✗		
Questioning	✗		✗	✗	✗			
Situational leadership	✗		✗	✗	✗			
Teambuilding			✗					
Knowledge								
Competitors/ customers	✗							

	Corporate goals	Own function	Roles of other functions	The business	Determination	Flexibility	Integrity	Empathy	Energy	Judgement	Courage
							X		X	X	X
							X	X	X	X	X
		X		X	X	X		X	X	X	
								X	X	X	
						X	X	X			
		X		X	X	X	X	X	X		X
	X	X	X	X	X	X		X	X	X	
	X	X	X	X				X	X	X	

Corporate goals
Own function
Roles of other
functions
The business

Attributes

Determination
Flexibility
Integrity
Empathy
Energy
Judgement
Courage

The answer to this question is that it is sometimes possible to add to skills and knowledge, but much harder to change personal attributes. Also, some go together. For example, it is hard to be a good coach if you have no feelings of empathy with the people you are coaching. Even when it may be possible to add an appropriate skill, time may not permit this. There is another way, and this is for the manager to find a partner who has the things that they lack. In our example, the partner would need more of the interpersonal skills than our manager possesses. By working together, they can supply all the things that are needed, provided each recognizes personal shortfalls and is willing to allow the other person to take the conceptual leadership in their weak areas.

Reading about change can only take you so far. Change management skills *need* to be exercised, and this book can only set you on the path. Use the ideas offered wisely.

FURTHER READING

Paul Bate (1994) *Strategies for Cultural Change*, Oxford, Butterworth Heinemann.

David Hussey (editor)(1996) *The Implementation Challenge*, Chichester, Wiley.

D E Hussey (editor) (1993) *International Review of Strategic Management*, Chichester, Wiley, pp 63-70.

Noel M Tichy and Mary Anne Devanna (1990) *The Transformational Leader*, New York, Wiley (originally published in 1986, republished 1990 with an additional preface).

INDEX